TOP BUSINESS THINKERS

"This small book will exequip you to thrive in an unpredictable future as much as any other book you might read. Its elements—images, stories, ideas, and cool related stuff—are masterfully woven together for maximum impact in minimum time." —Ben Sherwood, author of *The Survivors Club*

"This is superb learning technology for today's busy leaders and their busy organizations. Fun to read and easy to digest, it still packs one heck of a wallop." —Steve Kerr, former Vice President of Corporate Leadership Development and Chief Learning Officer, GE

"Every executive wishes for a way to make crucial business ideas and conversations into a framework for applying them to the everyday culture of the organization. These 'lenses' are one of the most effective tools I've encountered for doing that." —Michael Paxton, former President, Pillsbury Baked Goods and CEO of Haagen Dazs

"Once in a great while someone figures out how to transform the confusing complexity of the business world into beguiling simplicity, without losing anything in the translation. This delightful and intelligent book has that quality from cover to cover. Highly recommended!"—Steve Lundin, co-author of *Fish!* And *Top Performer*

"In a range of simple ways that will surprise you, this book has the power to turn the ordinary into the extraordinary and the extraordinary into the truly amazing." —Robert Cooper, author of the *BusinessWeek* best-seller *The Other 90%* and *Get Out of Your Own Way*

"SEE NEW NOW will provide you with an entire spectrum of new and effective ways to perceive the complex reality around us. It will enable you to see things differently in a way that can help you generate profitable ideas and approaches for your business, or for your family life. Its stories are sharp, edgy and memorable—they will stay with you for a long, long time." —Adrian Slywotzky, Managing Director of Oliver Wyman and author of *The Upside* and *Value Migration*

"Our universe, as a writer has said, is made not out of atoms but out of stories. The wonderful stories here will expand any reader's universe of perspectives, understandings, and possibilities." —Judith Delozier, co-author of *The Encyclopedia of Systemic Neuro-Linguistic Programming and NLP New Coding*

"SEE NEW NOW stimulates the creative spirit like very few other business books. It's a great way to start building a real culture of innovation in any organization." —Mark Johnson, chairman, Innosight, and co-author of *The Innovator's Guide to Growth*

"How we view the world sets the parameters for how we respond. Here Jerry de Jaager and Jim Ericson provide a wealth of new lenses through which to look, think, and act differently, both as business leaders and members of the new global community." —Dov Seidman, author of the *New York Times* best-seller *How: Why HOW We Do Anything Means Everything in Business (and in Life)*

SEE
NEW
NOW

NEW LENSES FOR LEADERSHIP AND LIFE

GERALD DE JAAGER
&
JAMES ERICSON

© 2009 All rights reserved. • Bergen Publishing LLC • www.seenewnow.com

ISBN-10: 0-615-31896-7
ISBN-13: 978-0-615-31896-7

"Insight lasts; theories don't. And even insight decays into small details, which is how it should be. A few details that have meaning in one's life are important." —Peter Drucker

"To do things differently, we must learn to see things differently. Seeing differently means learning to question the conceptual lenses through which we view and frame the world, our businesses, our core competencies, our competitive advantage, and our business models. It means finding new eyeglasses that will enable us to see strategies and structures taking shape, even if we feel that we are on the edge of chaos; it is a matter of survival in the new world of business." —John Seely Brown

CONTENTS

Introduction	1
The Scent on the Floor	5
The Baboon Reflex	11
The Balance Pole	17
The Bolero Challenge	25
The Homunculus	31
Signature Move	37
The Garden Path	41
The Louis Armstrong Effect	47
Figure and Ground	55
The Million-Dollar Parrot	61
Einstein's Compass	69
The Itsy Bitsy Spider	79
Bird-Brained Logic	83
Shooting David Petraeus	89
The Mile Run	97
Abwoon D'bwashmaya	103

The Insect-Size Buffalo	109
The Hedgehog and the Fox	115
The Puddle	125
The Fly in the Urinal	133
Spencer's Warbler	139
The Twenty-Dollar-Bill Auction	147
The Stirrup	153
The Caterpillar	161

ALSO AVAILABLE
at www.seenewnow.com

- ✓ Additional copies of the printed book. Discounted prices are available for volume purchases.
- ✓ The e-book of SEE NEW NOW, which includes over 150 activated hyperlinks that permit you to explore supplementary resources.
- ✓ Additional lenses created since the book was published (PDF files)
- ✓ Lens Expanders that will help you gain more from the lenses (PDF files)
- ✓ All individual lenses from SEE NEW NOW (PDF files)
- ✓ Copyright permissions for legally distributing downloaded material to others
- ✓ A site license to make all downloadable SEE NEW NOW content available to everyone in your organization—at a surprisingly low price

Introduction

Here you will find twenty-four brief stories that can help you think about your world differently. They're metaphors; they're thought-starters—we call them new lenses because they enable you to see familiar things in new ways.

The lenses can be temporary ways of turning on your fullest creativity as you do some especially important thinking, or they may create new perspectives that will permanently affect how you view things. They will lead to positive differences in the way you think and act—as a leader, as an innovator, and perhaps as a person.

Throughout an organization, they elevate the creativity and energy that individuals and teams bring to solving problems and finding opportunities. Moreover, because the titles of the lenses quickly become a shared, easily-recalled shorthand for important concepts, conversations about those concepts flourish more readily and are sustained more easily, embedding the search for better ideas into the everyday life of the organization.

In more than twenty years heading The Masters Forum, we have hosted presentations by more than 150 of the world's preeminent business thinkers.[1] Those exceptional men and women generally offer insightful solutions to organizational issues. We refer to many of their ideas in this book, but we take a different approach that is complementary to theirs, offering these lenses as twenty-four distinctive ways to help you find your own best ideas for any kind of issue you might be facing.

We believe that on your own you'll see plenty of applications for the lenses, from finding deep insights to simply perking up meetings. The primary benefits from using them arise from insights that are sparked, questions that are asked, constructive new conversations that probably would not have occurred otherwise, and the establishment of a shared vocabulary for new thinking. Openness to where they can take you is the most important quality for gaining the most from them.

Start anywhere. Something is bound to click, and soon you'll be seeing things in new ways that can yield great returns.

"Insight lasts; theories don't."
— Peter Drucker[2]

"If you get outside your own autobiography, you can learn. Animals learn only from their own experience; human beings can learn from the experiences of others, particularly if they can get outside their own head, their agenda, their background, their motive structure, and into the heads of other people." — Stephen Covey[3]

"I'm not yet as much of a learning person as I'd like to be. Like most Americans, I'm driven largely by an urge to perform, accomplish, achieve, and get things done. Yet as I begin to consciously shift to filtering everything through a learning lens, I find both dramatic and subtle differences in the way I do things and how I spend my time." — Jim Collins[4]

NOTES

1 Jerry de Jaager is education director of The Masters Forum; Jim Ericson is its founder and CEO. Among the speakers we have hosted are Peter Drucker, Malcolm Gladwell, Jim Collins, Tom Peters, Judith Bardwick, Gary Hamel, Meg Wheatley, Scott Adams, Rosabeth Moss Kanter, and Stephen Covey. Our website is www.mastersforum.com.

2 Quoted in Rubin, Harriet. "Peter's Principles." *Inc.* (March 1, 1998)

3 Covey, Stephen. "Seven Habits of Highly Effective People." Presentation at The Masters Forum (December 11, 1989)

4 Collins, Jim. "The Learning Executive." *Inc.* (August, 1997)

Image: "Spectacles" © Oakley, Julie. www.julieoakleydesign.com.

> Find many ideas, tips, and techniques for using and learning from the lenses at seenewnow.com

The Scent on the Floor

What you leave behind can help you or it can hurt you.

When Estée Lauder retired in 1994 as head of the cosmetics company that bears her name, she commanded a privately-held business empire that controlled 45 percent of the cosmetics market in American department stores, employed more than 10,000 people in 118 countries, and registered annual sales exceeding four billion dollars. Quite a journey for the woman born Josephine Esther Mentzer in New York City, who according to *Time* magazine "stalked the bosses of New York City department stores until she finally got some counter space at Saks Fifth Avenue in 1948."[1]

As her company grew, Lauder decided to expand internationally. In 1960, she succeeded in opening its first overseas outlet in one of London's top department stores, Harrods. From there, she anticipated success throughout Europe. "If I could start with the finest store in London, all the other great stores would follow," she said.[2]

But Paris was to prove more challenging than London. The perfume buyer at Galeries Lafayette, Paris's most prestigious department store, was disdainful of this upstart American woman with the made-up French-sounding first name. He refused even to meet with her.

After trying fruitlessly for several days to obtain an appointment, Lauder took matters into her own hands. She walked into the perfume section of Galeries Lafayette, uncapped a bottle of Youth Dew (her company's most successful perfume), turned it over, and emptied it onto the carpet.

Harvard Business School professor Nancy Koehn reported what happened next in her book, *Brand New*:

> Over two days, shoppers repeatedly asked Galeries Lafayette saleswomen where they could purchase the scent. Some of these conversations took place in the presence of the store's cosmetics buyer, who was impressed with women's enthusiasm for Youth Dew. Within a few weeks, Estée Lauder opened her first counter in Galeries Lafayette.[3]

In its most basic business application, this lens opens the following question: What scent does your company leave behind, and how does that affect your relationships with customers and others?

There was a time when this issue most commonly arose during

a scandal or crisis: Johnson & Johnson gained market share because of how it handled its Tylenol tampering crisis; Ford lost it as a result of the denials and disinformation it issued regarding its Pintos' combustible gas tanks.

But in today's increasingly transparent and connected world, the aftereffects of any company's internal and external interactions—its reputation: the scents it leaves behind—may be among the most important factors for achieving enduring success. So argues Dov Seidman in his bestselling 2007 book, *HOW*.[4] The influential columnist Thomas Friedman wrote about Seidman and incorporated Seidman's views into his own bestseller, *The World Is Flat*. In a column, Friedman explained:

> Seidman's simple thesis is that in this transparent world "how" you live your life and "how" you conduct your business matters more than ever, because so many people can now see into what you do and tell so many other people about it on their own without any editor. To win now, he argues, you have to turn these new conditions to your advantage.[5]

The scent Estée Lauder left behind lasted a few days and affected perhaps a few thousand shoppers, yet it was enough to transform her company's future. Today what you leave behind can reach millions in moments and endure in cyberspace for decades; its potential impact is inestimable.[6]

In 2008, the resignation of New York governor Eliot Spitzer captured the power of an unintended scent. The once-acclaimed exemplar of morality was tarnished; the once-powerful leader became a castoff. As one reporter put it, "He is a person who in one moment was transformed into his opposite."[7]

What are you leaving behind you, at work, at home, and elsewhere, today and in the long run? If you consider it as a scent, what's it like?

The Scent of Rain

from *How Stuff Works*[8]

[T]he smells people associate with rainstorms can be caused by a number of things. One of the more pleasant rain smells, the one we often notice in the woods, is actually caused by bacteria! *Actinomycetes*, a type of filamentous bacteria, grow in soil when conditions are damp and warm. When the soil dries out, the bacteria produces spores in the soil. The wetness and force of rainfall kick these tiny spores up into the air where the moisture after a rain acts as an aerosol (just like an aerosol air freshener)... The bacteria is extremely common and can be found in areas all over the world, which accounts for the universality of this sweet "after-the-rain" smell.

Another sort of smell is caused by the acidity of rain. Because of chemicals in the atmosphere, rainwater tends to be somewhat acidic, especially in urban environments. When it comes in contact with organic debris or chemicals on the ground, it can cause some particularly aromatic reactions. It breaks apart soil and releases minerals trapped inside, and it reacts with chemicals, such as gasoline, giving them a stronger smell. These reactions generally produce more unpleasant smells than bacteria spores, which is why the after-the-rain smell isn't always a good one.

Another after-the-rain smell comes from volatile oils that

plants and trees release. The oil then collects on surfaces such as rocks. The rain reacts with the oil on the rocks and carries it as a gas through the air. This scent is like the bacteria spores in that most people consider it a pleasant, fresh smell. It has even been bottled and sold for its aromatic qualities!

NOTES

1 Mirabella, Grace. "Estée Lauder: She Transformed Beauty into Big Business by Cultivating Classy Sales Methods and Giving Away Samples." ("The *Time* 100 Most Influential People of the Century") *Time* (December 7, 1998)

2 Koehn, Nancy. *Brand New: How Entrepreneurs Earned Customers' Trust from Wedgwood to Dell* (Boston: Harvard Business School Press, 2001)

3 Ibid.

4 Seidman, Dov. *HOW: Why HOW We Do Anything Means Everything … in Business (and in Life)* (New York: John Wiley, 2007)

5 Friedman, Thomas. "The Whole World Is Watching." *New York Times* (June 27, 2007)

6 For a thorough, wise, and practical account of what it takes to endow a company with the requisite systems and practices to retain its integrity, see Heineman, Ben, *High Performance with High Integrity (Memo to the CEO)* (Cambridge, MA: Harvard Business School Press, 2008). Heineman served as General Counsel at GE under CEOs Jack Welch and Jeffrey Immelt.

7 Samuels, David, interviewed by Brooke Gladstone. "Sweet and Lowbrow." *On the Media* (March 15, 2008) www.onthemedia.org

8 _____. "What Causes the Smell after Rain?" *HowStuffWorks* at www.howstuffworks.com

The Baboon Reflex

Fear makes animals, and people, do unproductive things.

Robert Sapolsky is a brilliant scientist with a knack for showing what humans can learn from animal behavior. His best-selling books include *Why Zebras Don't Get Ulcers* and *A Primate's Memoir*.[1]

A Stanford professor and winner of a MacArthur "genius" award, he conducts extensive first-hand research among baboons in Africa—he's been going there for more than 20 years. Here's a story he's told about baboon behavior:

> When baboons hunt together they'd love to get as much meat as possible, but they're not very good at it. The baboon is a much more successful hunter when he hunts by himself than when he hunts in a group because they screw up every time they're in a group. Say three of them are running as fast as possible after a gazelle, and they're gaining on it, and they're deadly. But something goes on in one of their minds—I'm anthropomorphizing here—and he says to himself, "What am I doing here? I have no idea whatsoever, but I'm running as fast as possible, and this guy is running as fast as possible right behind me, and we had one hell of a fight about three months ago. I don't quite know why we're running so fast right now, but I'd better just stop and slash him in the face before he gets me." The baboon suddenly stops and turns around, and they go rolling over each other like Keystone cops and the gazelle is long gone....[2]

Anything like that ever happen in your organization, or your life? Forgetting the team's goal and worrying instead about who might be gaining on you? These baboons had a goal and they had motivation to achieve it that's just about as powerful as any motivation could be: food and survival. In today's terms, they were "highly incented." But fear undermined them nonetheless.

Makes you think of W. Edwards Deming's famous pronouncement, "Drive out fear, so that everyone may work effectively for the company,"[3] doesn't it? "The economic loss from fear is appalling," Deming said.[4]

Back when AOL acquired Time Warner in 2001 and all the

experts were bowing down to this brilliant exercise in the most current business buzzword of the day, "synergy"—that was before the stock price lost 80 percent of its value and the whole enterprise eventually fell apart—one commentator saw the baboons. Under the headline "Reminder to Steve Case: Confiscate the Long Knives," *Wired* columnist Frank Rose cautioned that Time Warner had become "a corporate version of the Holy Roman Empire: a loose confederation of fiefdoms that are as likely to be at war with one another as with outsiders. Infighting can break out at any level..."[5]

Was it a long history of fear and jealousy that created that disastrous culture? Hard to know for sure, but what do you think?

The fear center in the human brain has a hair trigger. An experiment shows how exceptionally susceptible to fear we are. Brain scientists wired up some people as they were watching the 2006 Super Bowl, in order to see which brain parts were activated as the commercials were viewed. Federal Express introduced a commercial in which a caveman is reprimanded by his caveman boss for not using Federal Express to ship an important package. As the reprimanded caveman walks away from the encounter, he is stepped on and crushed by a dinosaur.

Most people might describe this ad as "funny" or "cute," not frightening, but to our brains, it's an entirely different matter. More particularly, it's deeply alarming to the brain's fear center, the amygdala, which seeks out danger and then issues warnings throughout the body's systems. Here's a chart of the amygdalar activity that those Super Bowl researchers measured among the viewers of that FedEx commercial, up to and just past the moment when the caveman gets crushed by the dinosaur (as indicated by the arrow):[6]

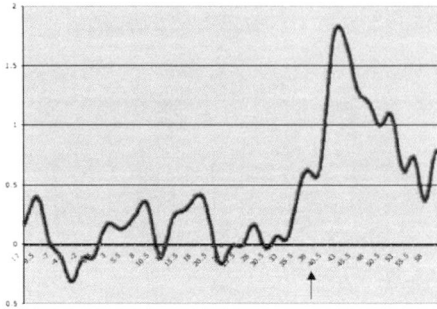

Fear is almost always with us, even when we're unaware of it. It might be easy to nod in wise agreement with the management shibboleth, "People don't dislike change; they just dislike being changed," but there's only a small amount of truth in that. Acknowledging the sharp, constant, often-hidden reality of fear is a crucial first step toward hushing the ancient brain centers that can turn even our best intentions into disappointments that only look like slapstick comedies to those who are not living them.

One Leader's Fear

Former publishing executive James Autry has written ten books about the human side of leadership. He begins his book *Life & Work* with a story that includes the following exchange between him and a friend:[7]

> "Do you ever get the feeling that one day they are going to come into your office and say, 'Okay, Autry, we found out about you'?"
>
> "Yes, yes," I said, almost shouting. "I frequently get that feeling. You, too?"
>
> He nodded, and we both began to laugh. "You know what this tells us," he continued.

I knew, but I could not find the exact words. He did it for me: "There are no big boys, only us little boys."

NOTES

1 Sapolsky, Robert. *Why Zebras Don't Get Ulcers* (New York: Holt, 2004); *A Primate's Memoir: A Neuroscientist's Unconventional Life among the Baboons* (New York: Scribner, 2004)

2 Sapolsky, Robert. "A Bozo of a Baboon: A Talk with Robert Sapolsky." at *Edge* (www.edge.org)

3 Deming, W. Edwards. *Out of the Crisis.* (Cambridge, MA: MIT Press, 2000)

4 Walton, Mary. *The Deming Management Method.* (New York: Perigee, 1988)

5 Rose, Frank. "Reminder to Steve Case: Confiscate the Long Knives." *Wired* (September, 2000)

6 Iacoboni, Marco. "Who Really Won The Super Bowl? The Story of an Instant-Science Experiment." at *Edge* (www.edge.org)

7 Autry, James. *Life & Work: A Manager's Search for Meaning* (Harlingen, TX: Quill Books, 1995)

Image source: ©istockphoto.com/alptraum

SEE NEW NOW

The Balance Pole

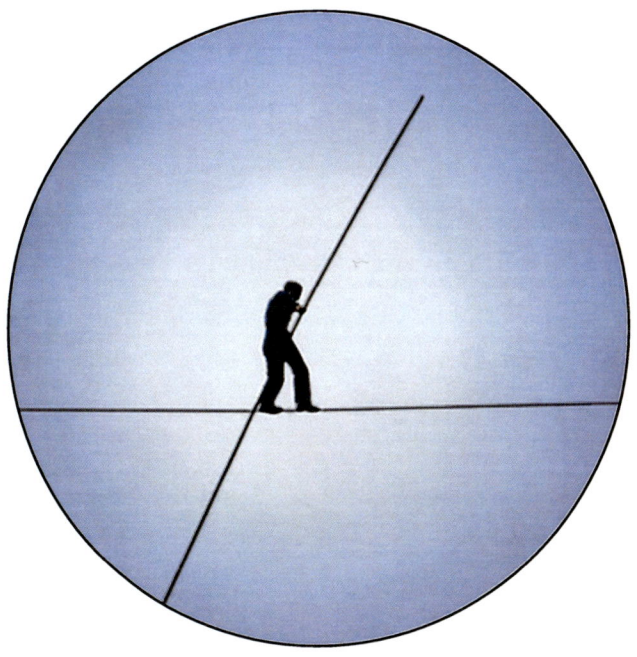

Hanging on to your tools in the wrong circumstances can have tragic results.

Karl Wallenda was the patriarch of a family of the world's greatest high-wire performers. He, along with a host of family members, invented and performed many stunning acts, such as the seven-person pyramid: four on the wire, two balanced on their shoulders, and the seventh seated in a chair above them. After premiering in Milan in 1925, the troupe was soon signed by John Ringling's "Greatest Show On Earth," where their first performance was met with a 15-minute standing ovation.[1] They never used a safety net.

"Life is being on the wire," Karl would say. "Everything else is just waiting." On March 22, 1978, at the age of 73, he was walking a high wire between two towers of a seaside hotel in Puerto Rico when a gust of wind threw off his balance. He crouched, then lost his balance again. He began to fall, grabbing for the wire with one hand while he held his 23-foot-long, 36-pound balance pole with the other. Unable to maintain his grip on the wire, he fell 120 feet to his death. His grandson said:

> People felt he could have saved himself if he had just dropped the pole. But he would never do that. He taught us never to drop the pole.[2]

Even the most useful tools have their limits, and knowing when to let go of them can make all the difference.[3]

Knockout strategies often let go of what others have considered indispensable elements. Southwest Airlines bypassed the hub-and-spoke system that its main competitors used; companies like Amazon and Netflix did away with the brick-and-mortar-based thinking that kept existing companies stuck in the past.

To choose just one example from today, the "free stuff revolution" means that large numbers of customers can pay nothing for items that include air travel, rental cars, international telephone calls, and daily newspapers—advertisers pick up the tab.[4] Europe's Ryanair, for example, which flies 190 airplanes among 140 destinations, carries about one-fourth of its passengers for free, and the CEO has declared a goal of increasing that fraction closer to one-half.[5]

Letting go of the age-old question, "How much will customers pay for this?" is the first step. Replacing it with "*Who* will pay for this?" comes next.

What tools are you, or your organization, hanging on to when they need to be let go? Elsewhere in this book (see "The Mile Run") we note that Clayton Christensen has recommended that companies need to drop, or at least reconfigure, some very precious tools of financial analysis if they want to truly stimulate powerful innovation. Adrian Slywotzky demonstrated in his book *The Upside* that Toyota might never have developed the Prius had it clung slavishly to its risk-assessment tools that told it that there was about a one in twenty chance of success for that venture.

More hair-raising for executives might be the outcomes of a 2008 conference that gathered many of the brightest business minds, academic and applied, of our day to consider two related questions:

> What is it about the way large organizations are currently managed that will most imperil their ability to thrive in the decades ahead; and given this, what fundamental changes will be needed in management principles, processes and practices?

Twenty-five "moonshots for management" emerged, each of which requires that some precious, hard-won tools be dropped by someone.[6]

At a more operational level, consider how industry leaders have dropped old tools and developed new, more effective ones. In hiring, for example, determining skill qualifications such as education and experience has long been an essential tool for employee selection. Yet Southwest Airlines spokesman Terry Millard says the rule at Southwest is "Hire for attitude, train for skill."[7] Southwest applies the rule even to pilots, according to Millard.

Regarding customer satisfaction, so much has been spent for so long on exhaustive, detailed surveys—yet Frederick Reichheld of Bain & Company argues that just one survey question—Would you recommend this company to a friend?—is all that's required to predict top-line growth in most circumstances:[8] General Electric, American Express, Intuit, and Procter & Gamble are among the companies that have dropped or modified older tools and picked up this one.[9]

What could be a more mundane, unquestioned tool than the invoice form? James Collins has hailed the California company Graniterock for adding the following words at the bottom of every invoice: "If you are not satisfied for any reason, don't pay us for it. Simply scratch out the line item, write a brief note about the problem, and return a copy of this invoice along with your check for the balance." In its new manifestation, the old invoice is not just a tool for collecting what's owed, it's a mechanism to drive customer satisfaction throughout the organization.

Graniterock refers to the policy as "short pay." Collins writes:

> To put the radical nature of short pay in perspective, imagine paying for airline tickets after the flight and having the power to short pay depending on your travel experience—not just in the air, but during ticketing and deplaning as well…. Or suppose your cell phone bill came with a statement that said, "If you are not satisfied with the quality of connection of any calls, simply identify and

deduct those from the total and send a check for the balance."[10]

For individuals, there is probably no tool more deeply ingrained in us than the complex of behaviors that we call "personality." Yes, personality is a tool: among other things, it's the mechanism we use to try to get what we want from life. Yet behind the most popular training programs of the last half-century—situational leadership, social styles, consultative selling, learning styles, and principled negotiation, to name just five—lies the premise that true effectiveness often will require a leader to "drop" the style he or she is most comfortable with and use other ones in order to build truly effective long-term relationships.

We all create "balance poles" to stabilize us and allow us to move forward during the high-wire act of making it through our lives and careers. Sometimes, when the wind shifts, just for a moment or maybe for the longer term, we need to let go of them.

Dropping the Wrong Tools

History is filled with examples of institutions and individuals dropping the wrong tools, for many reasons, including the glitter of faddish newer tools, misperceptions of what they really need, and just plain negligence. This is an excerpt from an address in October 2008 by former Federal Reserve chair Alan Greenspan.[11]

> Another important requirement for the proper functioning of market competition is also not often, if ever, covered in lists of factors contributing to economic growth and standards of living: trust in the word of others....

Wealth creation requires people to take risks, and thus we cannot be sure our actions to enhance our material wellbeing will succeed. But the greater our ability to trust in the people with whom we trade, that is, the more enhanced their reputation, the greater the accumulation of wealth. In a market system based on trust, reputation has a significant economic value. I am therefore distressed at how far we have let concerns for reputation slip in recent years.

Reputation and the trust it fosters have always appeared to me to be the core attributes required of competitive markets… When trust is lost, a nation's ability to transact business is palpably undermined. In the marketplace, uncertainties created by not always truthful counterparties raise credit risk and thereby increase real interest rates and weaker economies.

During the past year, lack of trust in the validity of accounting records of banks and other financial institutions in the context of inadequate capital led to a massive hesitancy in lending to them. The result has been a freezing up of credit.

NOTES

1 ____. "Sit Down, Poppy, Sit Down!" *Time* (April 3, 1978)

2 Gallagher, Peter. "Wired: For Sarasota's Flying Wallendas, The Thrill of Performing High in The Sky Triumphs over Family Tragedies." *Sarasota Magazine* (February, 2006)

3 The great business thinker Karl Weick introduced the term "Drop your tools" into management discourse in an essay reflecting on the deaths of a number of firefighters, where he wrote:
In both cases, these 23 men and four women were overrun by

exploding fires when their retreat was slowed because they failed to drop the heavy tools they were carrying. By keeping their tools, they lost valuable distance they could have covered more quickly if they had been lighter. All 27 perished within sight of safe areas. The question is, why did the firefighters keep their tools? The imperative, "drop your tools or you will die," is the image that I want to examine more closely…

Dropping one's tools is a proxy for unlearning, for adaptation, for flexibility, in short, for many of the dramas that engage organizational scholars. It is the very unwillingness of people to drop their tools that turns some of these dramas into tragedies.

See Weick, Karl, "Drop Your Tools: An Allegory for Organizational Studies," *Administrative Science Quarterly* (June, 1996).

4 "Free Love" (March, 2008) at Trendwatching.com

5 Ibid.

6 See Hamel, Gary, "Moonshots for Management," *Harvard Business Review* (February, 2009). Read more about the group and its conclusions in a series of blog posts by Hamel at http://www.managementlab.org/blog/2009/moonshots-managers.

7 Millard, Terry. "Greatness Is An Inside Job." Presentation at The Masters Forum (October 13, 2004). You can read this at www.seenewnow.com/summaries/millard.pdf.

8 Reichheld, Frederick. "The One Number You Need to Grow." *Harvard Business Review* (December, 2003). See his *The Ultimate Question* (Boston: Harvard Business School Press, 2006)

9 _____. "Would You Recommend Us?" *BusinessWeek* (January 30, 2006)

10 Collins, James. "Turning Goals Into Results: The Power of Catalytic Mechanisms." *Harvard Business Review* (July-August, 1999)

11 Greenspan, Alan. "Markets and the Judiciary." Address to the Sandra Day O'Connor Project at Georgetown University (October 2, 2008) See at www.law.georgetown.edu/news/documents/Greenspan.pdf

The Bolero Challenge

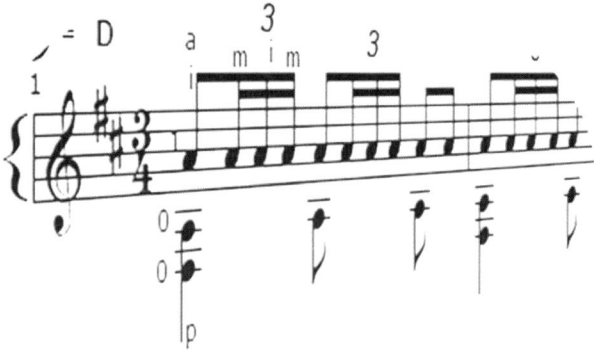

Great results require attention to the accompaniment, not just the melody.

Described as a "veritable hymn to desire" and an "exaltation of the erotic," Maurice Ravel's 1928 orchestral composition, *Bolero*, is reportedly the world's most frequently played piece of classical music.[1] It extended its reach into popular culture when it was used as the background music for Dudley Moore's tryst with Bo Derek in the movie *10*.

In an Oscar-winning documentary, the conductor of the Los Angeles Philharmonic Orchestra, Zubin Mehta, discussed the complexities of successfully performing *Bolero*. He said, "It's not only the melody that's important. The build-up is going on in the accompaniment as well as in the theme." Expanding, he said:

> The way *Bolero* builds up, it's not even comparable to any Beethoven or Brahms symphony ending, because those are normal, natural strettos [increases of musical intensity] at the end of movements. *Bolero*'s stretto starts from the first bar and continues. So keeping up the tempo, keeping up the pace and not going forward, not giving in to your instinct which pushes you forward—to hold this back, that is the tough part. I have seen performances of *Bolero* where the side drum, for instance, by the middle of the piece is already at its peak—you can't do anything about it. The conductor can't bring them down and build them back up again. It's got to be done very, very carefully.[2]

In your organization, what gets more attention, the theme or the accompaniment? Do the "background" things like fostering innovation, developing employees, strengthening core competencies, living your values, or even marketing have a proper rhythm in relation to such front-and-center "melodies" as sales and production, so that long-term goals and short-term activities come together in satisfying ways?

For many years, management experts have observed that "hard drives out soft"—measurable indicators commonly take precedence over less-tangible intentions. Recent developments such as the "balanced scorecard," which adds strategic non-financial performance measures to traditional financial metrics, can give managers and executives a more multifaceted view of organizational performance.[3]

Relatedly, it has frequently been demonstrated that the immediate will often drive out the longer-term. In his classic study, *The Nature of Managerial Work*, Henry Mintzberg showed that however much lip service organizations might pay to future-oriented activities, it is reacting to "hot news"—whatever urgent is happening right now—that more typically drives most managers' behavior.[4]

Venture capitalist Scott Maxwell makes an explicit musical analogy in his advice to entrepreneurs about balancing hard and soft, long-term and immediate, writing,

> Just as great marketers develop a marketing rhythm for their customers, great CEOs set the beat for the overall organization. I highlighted below an illustrative rhythmic beat that an expansion stage CEO could set for the overall organization. (Looks something like an EKG measurement of a heart beating, doesn't it? Perhaps this is why companies with a great rhythm seem to come alive?)[5]

CEO RHYTHMIC BEAT – BOARD PERSPECTIVE

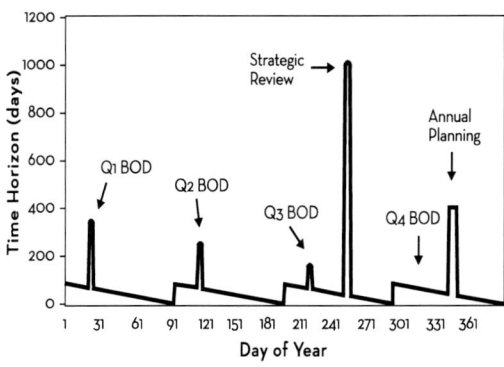

In 1972, Larry Greiner described longer-term organizational

rhythms in a *Harvard Business Review* article whose predictive power has been demonstrated time and time again, showing how one theme of company growth will always be dramatically, and inevitably, supplanted by another over time.[6] His model looked like this:

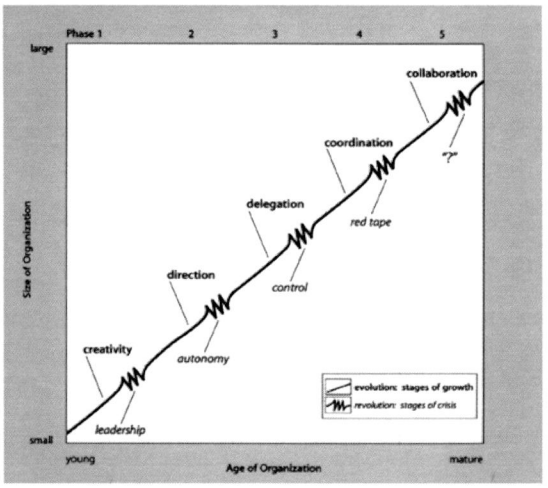

Because the "crises" in this depiction occur as a function of both the age of the organization and its size, the tempo of change will differ among organizations. The crises are similar to the strettos that Mehta discusses, places where overlapping themes (the growth stages) meet and must be integrated. Companies that manage toward an upcoming growth stage while focusing on the current one—that is, companies that attend to both the accompaniment and the theme—handle these transitions more easily.

The same kinds of issues occur, of course, in our personal lives. Retirement financial planning, for example, is a huge industry whose purpose is to help people pay sufficient attention to the "accompaniment"—building wealth—while they are concentrating on the "theme"—the financial decisions they make in the present moment. Effective career management may be said to have a similar rhythmic structure: developing aptitudes for desired future positions while also focusing on exemplary current performance.

"Beannacht" ("Blessing")

by John O'Donohue[7]

On the day when the weight deadens
on your shoulders
and you stumble
may the clay dance
to balance you.

And when your eyes
freeze behind
the gray window
and the ghost of loss
gets in to you,
may a flock of colours,
indigo, red, green
and azure blue,
come to waken in you
a meadow of delight.

When the canvas frays
in the curach of thought
and a stain of ocean
blackens beneath you,
may there come across the waters
a path of yellow moonlight
to bring you safely home.

May the nourishment of the earth be yours,
and the clarity of light be yours,

> may the fluency of the ocean be yours,
> may the protection of the ancestors be yours.
> And so may a slow
> wind work these words
> of love around you,
> an invisible cloak
> to mind your life.

NOTES

1 Henley, John. "Poor Ravel." *London Guardian* (April 25, 2001)

2 Fertik, William (director). *The Bolero.* (Pyramid Films, 1973). Available from First Run Features, New York. (www.firstrunfeatures.com)

3 See, for example, Rohm, Howard, "A Balancing Act," at www.balancedscorecard.org

4 Mintzberg, Henry. *The Nature of Managerial Work* (Englewood Cliffs, NJ: Prentice Hall, 1980)

5 Maxwell, Scott. "Is That You Humming?" *Now What?* (January 2, 2006) at http://scottmaxwell.wordpress.com

6 Greiner, Larry. "Evolution and Revolution As Organizations Grow." *Harvard Business Review* (May-June, 1972)

7 O'Donohue, John. *Anam Cara: A Book of Celtic Wisdom* (New York: HarperCollins, 1997). A "curach," O'Donohue told his audience when he read this poem at The Masters Forum in 2004, is "a kind of canvas canoe." You can hear him recite this poem at http://speakingoffaith.publicradio.org/programs/john_odonahue/ss_beannacht/ss-beannacht.shtml

The Homunculus

Sensing things wrongly is built into us.

Bob Toski is one of golf's great teachers, author of five instruction books on that subject. He once told an interviewer that the secret of his teaching success lay in understanding the homunculus:

> A natural swing produces a slice. That's because the homunculus, the part of the brain that controls motor movement, sees the hands as the largest part of your anatomy.... [W]hen the day comes to play golf, the instinct to move your hands away from you really takes over. On the downswing the

hands move away from the body too soon, out toward the target line, and you end up cutting across the ball from out to in. Thanks to the homunculus, I make a very good living.[1]

The homunculus isn't an actual part of your brain, but rather a depiction of what you look like to your brain based on how much of your brain's capacity is devoted to each part of your body. The image at the beginning of this lens illustrates the homunculus. Your hands, lips, and face are much better represented in your brain than most of the rest of your body. More brain cells are devoted to one thumb, for example, than to the entire back.[2] (In mice, the whiskers and snout take up most of the sensory brain space, whereas monkey brains dedicate large areas to the feet. That's evolution for you.)

Much as the ability to execute a good golf swing is impaired by the brain's over-recognition of the hands and under-recognition of the trunk and legs, imbalanced inputs to the corporate "brain" get in the way of organizational performance.

If you drew a picture of your organization based on the inputs it seeks and deals with and the ones that have a hard time getting recognized and addressed, what would that picture look like? Would it look that way because it's proper, or just because of evolution? Consultant Roger Martin argues, "The most exasperating fact about big companies in crisis is that they got there by doing what once made them big."[3]

Harvard Business School professor Robert Simons has similarly observed that what has been said of armies may also apply to companies: they are often very ready to fight the last war, but unprepared for the next one. In articles and books, Simons has shown how often control systems fail to capture all the current data that decision makers ought to have, because those systems are designed for yesterday, not today. For example, systems and practices established to take advantage of boom times can hamper adaptation to downturns.[4]

Speaking at The Masters Forum in 2007, information technology expert Jeffrey Sampler urged that organizations have to develop new sensory skills to compete effectively in an environment of rapid change and competitive threats that can appear seemingly out of nowhere. "How many people have a mental model that's incorrect? You think you understand the way the world works, based on your working data, and you make decisions based on that data, but the data may be totally inaccurate," he said.[5] Among other things, he asked:

> Do you have real-time customer profitability data down to the second decimal place?
>
> Do you have accurate, granular cost data that capture not only direct cost but indirect cost? You'll have to make some fairly precise cuts, and you must know that.

If an organization is not as sensitively attuned to those data as we are to our lips or fingertips, Sampler was saying, it will be in trouble.

You might add issues of your own to the ones Sampler noted. In a major survey, only 23 percent of companies said they had a systematic way of identifying what knowledge needed to be protected and retained for the company to remain fully competitive.[6] Two major 2007 studies of boards of directors reported that directors felt that they lacked adequate knowledge of vital strategic and operational information regarding the overall health of the organization.[7]

In the first lines of his book, *Evolution of Consciousness*, Stanford professor Robert Ornstein writes, "The mind is a squadron of simpletons. It is not unified, it is not rational, it is not well designed—or designed at all. It just happened, an accumulation of innovations of the organisms that lived before us."[8] Organizations can be like that, too, unless those in charge remember the homunculus.

Get it right, and an organization can develop the same sensing ability as Erik Weihenmayer, the first blind climber to scale Mount Everest: "His hands are like antennae, gathering information as they flick outward, surveying the rock for cracks, grooves, bowls, nubbins, knobs, edges and ledges, converting all of it into a roadmap etched into his mind."[9]

Experience the Homunculus
from "They Do It with Mirrors" by Helen Phillips[10]

There are a few simple illusions that demonstrate the amazing malleability of the brain's image of the body. One trick is to sit at a table and recruit a helper. Hide one hand under the table, resting palm down on your knee. Then ask your helper to tap, touch and stroke with their fingertips the back of your hidden hand and the table top directly above the hand with an identical pattern of movements, for a minute or two.

It's important that you concentrate on the table, where your helper is touching, and that you can't see your hand or their hand under the table. The more irregular the pattern, and the more synchronized the touches you can see and feel, the more likely you are to feel something very strange. About half the people who try this find that the table starts to feel like part of their body—as though the hand is transferred into the table.

NOTES

1 "My Shot: Bob Toski" *Golf Digest* (August, 2002)

2 Rubin, John. "Brain Changes." *Psychology Today* (March, 1989)

3 Martin, Roger. "Changing the Mind of the Corporation." *Harvard Business Review* (November-December, 1993)

4 See, for instance, the following works by Simons: "Control in an Age of Empowerment" *Harvard Business Review Classics* (April 15, 2001); "How Risky Is Your Company?" *Harvard Business Review* (May-June, 1999); and (with Robert Kaplan and Antonio Davila) *Performance Measurement and Control Systems for Implementing Strategy* (Englewood Cliffs, NJ: Prentice Hall, 1999)

5 Sampler, Jeffrey. "Ten Commandments for Competing in Turbulent Times." Presentation at The Masters Forum (March 20, 2007). You can read a summary of this presentation at www.seenewnow.com/summaries/sampler.pdf

6 _____. "Monster Study Reveals Employees Not Adequately Prepared for Impending 'Brain Drain'." *Business Wire* (September 25, 2007). Read the study at http://hiring.monster.com/hr/hr-best-practices/workforce-management/hr-knowledge-management/knowledge-retention-brain-drain.aspx

7 Kiefer, Rainier, Frank Mattern, and Frank Scholz. "The State of the Corporate Board 2007: A McKinsey Global Survey." *The McKinsey Quarterly* (April 2007); and *In the Dark II: What Many Boards and Executives Still Don't Know About the Health of their Business.* (Deloitte Touche Tohmatsu, 2007)

8 Ornstein, Robert. *Evolution of Consciousness: The Origins of the Way We Think* (New York: Simon & Schuster, 1992)

9 Greenfeld, Karl. "Blind to Failure." *Time Asia* (June 18, 2001)

10 Phillips, Helen. "They Do It with Mirrors." *New Scientist* (June 17, 2000)

Image source: Derived from an image by Chudler, Eric, at *Neuroscience for Kids* (http://faculty.washington.edu/chudler/brainsize.html)

Signature Move

What word, phrase, or image sums up your organization?

The hockey great Brett Hull was fielding questions at a youth hockey camp. One of the youngsters asked what quality was most important for making it to the National Hockey League. Hull answered:

> You have to be good, of course, so master the basics. But you also have to get noticed. There are thousands and thousands of kids like you out there who want to become pros.

Most of you will be lost in the crowd. The way to get the scouts to remember you is to develop a signature move—something you do so well that whenever your name is mentioned, everyone will have a picture of you in their mind.

Hull's own signature move was a sizzling, hundred-plus-mile-per-hour slap shot that some experts have ranked among the best ever.[1]

With people and with companies as with aspiring hockey stars, a signature move affects how you are thought of, how you are remembered, and how others react to you. So, signature move is one lens through which we can look at what we're doing, and perhaps think about how to do it differently.

We expect attentive service when we shop at Nordstrom, and we expect prompt delivery when we order a pizza from Domino's or ship a package by Federal Express. It's not accidental that we have those expectations: these companies spend a lot of money making sure that's how we think of them, and even more money making sure that we get what we expect. Lousy service at your local dollar store? What did you expect? Lousy service at Nordstrom? You feel like you've been cheated, and you might not go back.

A signature move isn't always a positive thing. Your internet service provider might provide generally excellent high-speed connections, but you might still view its signature move as something much slower, slothlike even: keeping you on hold forever when you call with a question; routing you through a voicemail maze before you can get any attention at all; making you wait too long for an installation or service appointment.

An advertising executive describes a client interaction:

> I was looking to try to identify what makes them unique. Their website and collateral material basically said that they did everything. It was just a bunch of blah blah. I brought up the "Signature Move," explaining to them that they needed a key differentiator. What makes them unique compared to other companies who do the same thing as they do? When I mention your company to your customers or prospects, what is the first thing that comes to mind? Those "Signature Move" questions moved us off dead center and really resonated.[2]

The signature moves we ascribe to people we work with are a shorthand way of characterizing perceived strengths and weaknesses. "She doesn't say much in meetings, but when she does, it's really valuable." "He's always glancing at his watch when you talk to him." "She steals the credit for any good ideas you give her." What's your signature move at work? What would you like it to be?

Of course, you have a signature move in your personal relationships, too. It might not be what you think it is; maybe it's not even what you'd hope it would be. Maybe it's better. Ask.

A Father's Signature Move

When business speaker Paul Stoltz came to The Masters Forum, he already had given hundreds of lectures around the world, but his father, who lived in Minneapolis, had never heard him speak to a group. So, we invited his father. Toward the end of his presentation, Stoltz asked his father to stand, introduced him to the audience, and said this:

> I don't know of a person who is more giving, on a 24/7 basis, than my father. He doesn't know how not to be giving. As a matter of fact, the coveted thing to happen in your life is to make the Gary Stoltz List. If you hit that list, you will be sent the coolest stuff, at the weirdest times. He just finds stuff—especially now that he's semi-retired—he finds stuff and sends it to the list. And then we all talk to each other: "Did you get that?" "Yeah, it was great!" "He's incredible! How does he find such great stuff?" I would say the ratio of give to get for my father is probably fifty to one.[3]

NOTES

1 See, for example, Conner, Floyd, *Hockey's Most Wanted: The Top 10 Book of Wicked Slap Shots, Bruising Goons, and Ice Oddities* (Dulles, VA: Potomac Books, 2002), where Hull's slap shot is rated as the fifth-best ever.

2 Personal communication from Jared Roy, President, Risdall Integration Group, Minneapolis, MN

3 Stoltz, Paul. "Stress-Hardiness." Presentation at the Masters Forum (December 10, 2002)

Image: "Power." © Johansson, Henrik. See more at www.flickr.com/blpz

The Garden Path

Our brains hate being misled.

Fat people eat accumulates.
The man who hunts ducks out on weekends.
The man who whistles tunes pianos.

All perfectly understandable sentences, right—at least once your brain has overcome its irritation and helped you figure them out.

They're called "garden-path sentences," for obvious reasons, and your brain does not like being led down this garden path: electrodes record furious increases in brain activity when readers reach the ends of such sentences. (For more, see note 1.)

No wonder! Think of all the work your brain has to do in order to provide you, instantaneously, with a sense of where a sentence is heading. In the examples above, you were probably ready, at least in a general sense, for what might come next. Fat people eat *too much*, or eat *lots of carbohydrates*. The man who whistles tunes *is very happy* . . .

We don't read the whole sentence and then figure it out; we gather its meaning and intent as we go along, with each word or word group. We're used to certain trustworthy syntactical forms that help us speed through each sentence correctly, not the use of those forms to pull the rug out from under us.

Many optical illusions make use of the same kinds of brain processes, applying a kind of jujitsu to what we've learned about the common relationships among things. The same goes for jokes, which often rely on subverting the reality established in the joke's premise.

Busy, busy, busy, our brains constantly rely on rules they already have learned, so we don't have to pause to figure everything out the way most of us have to do with those garden-path sentences.

This is true in a larger, organizational sense also. We learn what companies are about—their products and markets if we're consumers; their mission, values, and practices if we're employees—and we expect them to be true to that. That's the whole point of branding, for example—to establish a strong, consistent story in customers' minds.

Here's a garden-path headline from March 2008: "Victoria's Secret Chief Says Brand is Too Sexy." Huh? But it's for real.[2] After some disappointing financial performance, the company's CEO announced, "I feel so strongly about us getting back to our heritage and really thinking in terms of ultra-feminine and not just the word sexy." A superficial search-engine inquiry shows the words "Victoria's Secret" and "sexy" linked over four million times, whereas "Victoria's Secret" and "ultra-feminine" appear together about eleven thousand times. That's a lot of brain-rewiring the company will have to undertake.

In more poignant ways, organizations and their leaders play garden-path tricks on employees all the time. They state their values boldly, and promulgate them widely—only to behave inconsistently with them the same afternoon. They say they want "leadership," or "risk-taking," or "thinking outside the box," and then squelch people who do those things. Heck, organizational inconsistencies have helped Scott Adams and his "Dilbert" comic strip to rip-roaring success since 1989.

By now, many people have become so cynical about organizational integrity that they don't let their brains go to the trouble of constructing the stories their organizations would like them to believe. But there's still no question that people generally want to believe, and want an organization they can believe in. Speaking at the Masters Forum in 2008, Joseph Fuller, CEO of the international consulting firm Monitor Group, observed, "The institutions that last are those that have an enduring moral purpose":

> The important thing is that the purpose of the company and the purpose of your work are clear; they're reinforced by the metrics, they're reinforced by the strategy; no one is covering anything up... High-performing organizations have a very clear moral purpose: a very clear idea about the way they create value in the world and why that lends dignity to the work of the people who are there.[3]

As you communicate with employees, customers, and other stakeholders, are you setting forth a reliable moral purpose, or leading them down a garden path?

Stephen Covey's work, among others, offers many suggestions for personal-life applications of this lens: for example, to create a personal or family mission statement that is then prominently posted and regularly referred to as decisions are made, so there is a reliable consistency, a core "story" that family members can tell themselves about the unit they belong to. The commentator Dennis Prager has suggested a core question for parents to ask themselves, from which they might more consistently guide their actions: "Above all, if you have to choose, do you want your child to be successful, smart, happy, or good." (For Prager, "good" is the correct answer.)[4]

Covey has told the story of a corporate CEO who one day took a promising young employee out for a drive. Parking at the peak of a large hill with a sweeping vista below, the CEO asks the young person to step out of the car and look around. The CEO says: "Look at that; get a view of that land down there, get a view of that little stream down there, how it meanders. It's all private; it's wooded; you're only about seven minutes from the office. Twenty-five acres: I know how you and your family love to play games, tennis and all that. Imagine what you can do with all that beautiful land! We just want you to know that if you continue with your devotion, your loyalty, just like you've been giving it—even increase it if at all possible, even though we know how hard you're going—then four or five years from now, six years at the very most, all of that will be mine."[5]

Garden-path joke, or garden-path truth?

Language and Communication

from "Captain Cook's Porpoises" by Kenneth Norris[6]

[I]n all my work with porpoises I have never seen any evidence that suggests to me that they have a language like ours. I'm not surprised about this, either, since our strange method of acoustic communication is almost grotesquely clumsy and difficult. What other creature, for example, would want to wait around for the message involved in a long sentence; to wait until all the little abstract symbols like prepositions and adverbs and participles were arranged according to an arcane plan before meaning could be extracted?...

Purely as a prediction, I suggest that when we truly understand the sounds of porpoises and their meanings, we will have found that they have incredibly refined capability at 'seeing with sound,' to the point that they form sonic images of their environment. Further, it is already clear that they can hear the composition and texture of objects around them. I suspect they look into each other in eerie ways, inspecting the contours of internal air spaces like lungs and upper respiratory tract spaces, and that information about emotional states is to be gathered this way, even though the external surface of the animal is smooth and expression-free, having been dictated largely by the demands of hydrodynamics.

NOTES

1 Here are some more garden-path sentences:
   When Fred eats food gets thrown.
   The girl told the story cried.
   I convinced her children are noisy.
   She told me a little white lie will come back to haunt me.
   The dog that I had really loved bones.
   The raft floated down the river sank.
   We painted the wall with cracks.

2 Associated Press. "Victoria's Secret Chief Says Brand is Too Sexy." *International Herald Tribune* (March 2, 2008)

3 Fuller, Joseph. "Critical Threats and Opportunities in Business Today." Presentation at The Masters Forum (February 12, 2008) You can read a summary of this presentation at www.seenewnow.com/fuller_and_kerr.pdf

4 See Prager, Dennis, *Happiness is a Serious Problem: A Human Nature Repair Manual* (New York: Harper, 1998)

5 Covey, Stephen. "Seven Habits of Highly Effective People." Presentation at The Masters Forum (December 11, 1989)

6 Norris, Kenneth. "Captain Cook's Porpoises," in Stewart, Frank, ed., *A World Between Waves* (Washington, D.C.: Island Press, 1992)

Image: "The Curved Garden Path." © Simmonds, Jackie. See more at www.jackiesimmonds.com

The Louis Armstrong Effect

Louis Armstrong

Charles Black

Your impact on others can change the world.

Charles Black, who died in 2001, was remembered as "a man whose life affirmed the possibility of social progress," who had possessed "perhaps the most elegant legal mind of the modern era."[1] Before he began a 35-year career as a law professor at Yale and Columbia, he worked alongside Thurgood Marshall in crafting the arguments in *Brown v. Board of Education*, the 1954 case that declared racial segregation in public schools unconstitutional.

Black often told about the incident that shaped his life—hearing the jazz great Louis Armstrong play in a hotel ballroom in Austin, Texas in 1931, when Black was 16. "Armstrong was the first genius I had ever seen," he later wrote, adding:

> It is impossible to overstate the significance of a sixteen-year-old Southern boy's seeing genius, for the first time, in a black. We literally never saw a black then in any but a servant's capacity. It was just then that I started walking to the *Brown* case where I belonged.[2]

"Since that evening, October 12, 1931," Black later stated, "Louis Armstrong has been a continuing presence in my life."[3]

At the law schools where he taught, Black hosted an annual "Louis Armstrong Evening" to commemorate the day he encountered the jazz genius. Yale's dean recalled, "I can still see Charles in the faculty lounge, surrounded by a pile of 78s and a group of truly amazed students, talking about Louis Armstrong with the same appreciation with which he talked about John Marshall."[4]

One former student, Akhil Amar, now himself a law professor at Yale, said: "He was my hero. So many of the great moral issues of the 20th century seem clear in retrospect, but were quite controversial at the time. He had the moral courage to go against his race, his class, his social circle."[5] Another former student, who became dean of the University of Hawaii Law School, credited Black with inspiring a "ceaseless quest for justice."[6] Judge Guido Calabresi, who serves on America's second-highest court, wrote, "I still sit at his feet; he shapes my teaching, my thinking, and my judicial opinions every day."[7]

From one generation to the next and on to the next, Charles Black's life is affecting the theory and practice of law.

You never know how the flourishing of your own genius might affect others, but if there's one thing we know from contemporary science, it's that everything has some effect on the whole. As Jane Roberts has written, "You are so part of the world that your slightest action contributes to its reality. Your breath changes the atmosphere. Your encounters with others alter the fabrics of their lives, and the lives of those who come in contact with them."[8]

In business, interactions between people with different perspectives are crucial for innovation. A study of the top fifty game-changing innovations over a hundred-year period showed that nearly 80 percent of those innovations were sparked by someone whose primary expertise was outside the field in which the innovation breakthrough took place.[9] Intellectual Ventures, a Seattle-area company that brings together experts in unrelated fields to brainstorm marketable new ideas, files over five hundred patents per year; in 2008, the company had a backlog of three thousand additional patentable concepts.[10] Scott Anthony, president of the innovation consulting firm Innosight, has observed, "If you want one tip about how to encourage innovation in your company, it is to encourage intersections—to have people come together who will look at problems from different perspectives."[11]

We can't know whether Louis Armstrong might have imagined that his music would lead to change in the American civil-rights landscape, and in the way the law would be understood and implemented for generations to come. No one really knows what the effects of the way they live and work are going to be. But there will be some effects, of that you can be certain.

The Ward Attendant

The life of Helen Keller inspired millions of people, and changed the world. She was the first deaf and blind person to graduate from college. Her accomplishments, achieved through the guidance of her teacher Anne Sullivan, revolutionized the way deaf and blind children were taught.[12] Mark Twain said that Keller and Napoleon were the two most important figures of his century.

When Sullivan went to teach Keller, Keller was almost uncontrollably belligerent. Later Keller would call Sullivan (often called "Annie" Sullivan) "the light and beauty of my life."

Who was Anne Sullivan, and how did she become the person she was? The following is from a talk given at The Masters Forum in 1988 by Dr. Otis Maxfield:

> In my resident days, they sent me to Tewksbury State Hospital. I was there to do therapy, so I started seeing patients. After a session, I found myself locked in the ward. I started banging on the door and calling for help. Finally, a ward attendant, whose job was to take meals to patients, pick up trays, clean bathrooms—that sort of thing—came to let me out. This lady

was a pistol. She had been there forty years. She asked if she could help me in some way. I said I was going to start running some group sessions and could use some help doing it. She didn't like the idea very much. She said, "These people are nuts." She volunteered to sit in anyway.

In the first session, after I asked if anyone wanted to speak, a woman in back said she heard a voice. I said it wasn't a voice, it was me. With that, she picked up a book and hurled it at me. The ward attendant reached out and caught it just like she was playing left field. Then she said, "That's okay Mary. Tell us what the voice is telling you." I was both impressed and dismayed; I spent ten years learning how to do therapy and this wise old lady understood it better than I did.

At the end of my residency, I asked her to dinner because I had learned as much from her as I had from my high-priced formal education. She agreed, and we decided to leave directly from work the next day. Time came, and on the way out, she decided to take me on a tour of an underground cellblock, where she said they used to keep the violent patients.

The place was awful; it was cold and dark; water was dripping from the ceiling; rats were scurrying around. Thankfully, it had been abandoned years before. Halfway down the corridor, she pushed against a rusty gate and said, "This is where Annie lived." I asked her to tell me about Annie, and she told me an incredible story. She said "Annie came here as a kid and was crazy as a bedbug. They gave up on her after she tried to commit suicide and put her in this cell."

She continued, "In those days, my job was to serve three meals a day in the cellblock, but they told me I had to stay and feed Annie because she might kill herself if I left her alone with a knife and fork." She did that for a couple of months and decided it was useless. She said Annie wouldn't eat much and was slowly starving herself. One day she said, "Annie, this is ridiculous. Here's the fork and spoon. Do what you have to do." Annie began to eat. Then she said, "Why would a pretty girl like you try to kill herself?" From that day on, she and Annie visited three times a day.

During this same time frame, they discovered that Annie had contracted syphilis; she had lost her eyesight as a result. In spite of knowing that this was the crux of her problem, the staff still considered her to be a disturbed, dangerous young woman. Annie, however, began to get better. To talk. To walk. To sing. To play.

About that time, Perkins Institute for the Blind opened its doors in Boston. They contacted Tewksbury to find out if they had anyone there who could be trained to be productive in spite of their handicap. Tewksbury recommended Annie and she became part of their first class. She went on to be a great student. On the day of her graduation, the headmaster called her into his office and told her he had a great opportunity for her. He said there was a man in the waiting room that had a daughter who was a vegetable; she was blind and deaf and others had recommended that he have her institutionalized. But the man had other ideas and thought that if he could find someone to care for her it might make a difference. Annie took the job.

Annie Sullivan went on to be the lifelong companion of Helen Keller. Years later, Helen was asked to whom she owed the most. Helen Keller said, very simply, "I owe it all to Annie Sullivan, who taught me how to love and be loved."

It's a great story. But to me, the real story is the untold tale of a lady whose circumstances made her a ward attendant instead of the missionary she truly wanted to be, and who did what she could where those circumstances put her and forever changed the lives of an unbelievable number of people. Whenever I think I can't really help set people free, I try to remember that if this old gal could do it, then I should not give up now.

NOTES

1 Lazarus, Edward. "Charles Black: Elegy for a Heroic Lawyer." (May 15, 2001) at *FindLaw* http://writ.news.findlaw.com/lazarus/20010515.html

2 Hentoff, Nat. "Remembering a Great American." *Jewish World* (December 24, 2001)

3 Pollak, Louis. "Charles L. Black, Jr. and Civil Rights." *The Yale Law Journal* (June, 2002).

4 Kronman, Anthony. "The Genius of Charles Black." *The Yale Law Journal* (June, 2002). See also the reminiscence of Black's daughter, Robin Black: "In Memoriam—Charles L. Black, Jr." *Columbia Law Review* (May, 2002)

5 McFadden, Robert. "Charles L. Black Jr., 85, Constitutional Law Expert Who Wrote on Impeachment, Dies." *New York Times* (May 8, 2001)

6 Soifer, Aviam, "Charles L. Black, Jr.: Commitment, Connection and the Ceaseless Quest for Justice." *Asian-Pacific Law and Policy Journal* (Winter, 2006)

7 Calabresi, Guido. "Charles Black: Gentle Genius." *The Yale Law Journal* (June, 2002).

8 Roberts, Jane. *Adventures in Consciousness* (Needham, MA: Moment Point Press, 1984)

9 Jewkes, John, David Sawers and R. Stillerman. *The Sources of Invention* (New York: Macmillan, 1958)

10 Gladwell, Malcolm. "In the Air: Who Says Big Ideas Are Rare?" *The New Yorker* (May 12, 2008)

11 Anthony, Scott. "Putting Disruptive Innovation to Work." Presentation at The Masters Forum (April 16, 2008). You can read a summary of this presentation at www.seenewnow.com/summaries/anthony_and_johnson.pdf. See his book, co-authored with Mark Johnson and others, *The Innovator's Guide to Growth: Putting Disruptive Innovation to Work* (Boston: Harvard Business School Press, 2008)

12 "Anne Sullivan" at the website of The Perkins School for the Blind: www.perkins.org/culture/helenkeller/sullivan.html

Figure and Ground

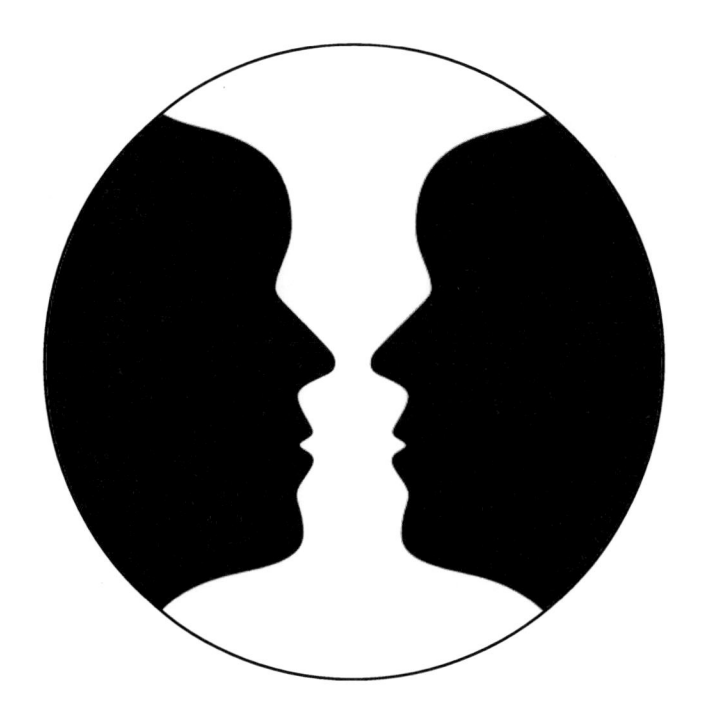

Shifting your focus lets you see much more.

All perception depends on differentiation. One of the first things a beginning artist learns is how to use line, color, shading, and other qualities to distinguish different elements in a work. An object that is emphasized is called the "figure"; everything else is called "ground." In the image above, a white chalice might be seen as the figure on a black ground, or you might see two profiled faces on a white ground. Note that it is virtually impossible to see both elements—the chalice and the faces—at the same time.

In general, we filter the huge amounts of sensory information we encounter by bringing parts of it into the foreground and ignoring or at least paying far less attention to the rest. In psychology, those kinds of differentiations are also referred to as figure and ground distinctions.

Important business ideas can result from switching figure and ground. Edith Weiner, president of Weiner Edrich Brown, a leading marketing consulting group, told a Masters Forum audience about a retailer's plans to publish a catalog of arthritis-related products. Because older women make up 63 percent of the market for such products, the company planned to put an appealing older woman on the catalog cover. That would have been a mistake, Weiner said, because by focusing on the *figure*—the 63 percent— the retailer could have lost much of the business of the rest of the arthritis population—the *ground*, in this case—because younger men and women are not likely to shop from a catalog with an older woman on the cover.

Better, Weiner said, would be to place people from the ground on the cover: an attractive middle-aged man, a younger woman, and a child. Older women and men with arthritis would still shop from that catalog, but other demographics would see that it was for them, too.[1]

Weiner urged her Masters Forum audience, "Get your team together and ask what assumptions you're making about figure and ground. Then switch them and see what happens. Just do it. I guarantee you—you'll see light bulbs going off all over the place."

In an attempt to cause his company's employees to keep financial performance in the foreground instead of the background, the legendary Silicon Valley entrepreneur Renn Zaphiropoulos once called a meeting in his company's parking lot and then rode around on an elephant with the company's financials prominently displayed on its sides while the Stanford University marching band played accompaniment.[2]

In his 2007 book, *The Upside*, Adrian Slywotzky invites business decision-makers to occasionally turn their attention away from the constant figure preoccupations of threat and risk and to see the great opportunities for growth in the ground around that threat and risk.[3] He told a Masters Forum audience, "Businesses shouldn't think of risk as only a negative. They need to recognize that it's an unconventional but very effective way to find growth opportunities."[4]

For example, when Target strategists studied future possibilities, Wal-Mart always loomed as a huge threat—the figure in all Target's planning. By looking beyond direct competition with Wal-Mart to the larger ground around it, Target saw the niche it came to occupy, as an "upscale discounter" to customers who were looking for Wal-Mart-like discounts but would pay extra for style.

Making what previously was ground for consumers into figure instead can become an important source of differentiation. Also using Target as an example, author Daniel Pink showed his Masters Forum audience a designer toilet brush sold at Target for $5.99, making the point that affluence permits consumers to select for design as well as functionality and buy Target's brush instead of a less-expensive alternative.[5] But it can also be noted that to care about the design of a toilet brush, the purchaser must see it not as mere insignificant *ground* in the bathroom setting, virtually or actually invisible, but as noticeable *figure*, and therefore important enough to spend extra money on.

In our personal lives as well, shifting figure and ground can influence what we think and what we do. We make to-do lists to remind us of what should be front and center in our attention and what should be background. Many couples find that what they thought was going to be the figure in their relationships turns out to be ground: "Cookin' lasts, kissin' don't" is one pithy way of expressing that shift. Other common expressions such as "Too busy earning a living to really make money," and "Many more fish in the sea," also rely for their impact on switching figure and ground.

So, try Edith Weiner's recommended exercise at work or at home. You might discover some very interesting new grounds for improvement.

The Spotlight of Attention

From "Magic and the Brain: Teller Reveals the Neuroscience of Illusion" by Jonah Lehrer[6]

After describing a trick performed by the illusionists Penn and Teller in which an audience member fails to notice many changes taking place around him because his attention has been directed elsewhere, the author writes:

> "The idea for this trick came straight from science," Teller says. "We thought it would be fun to show people how bad they are at noticing stuff." Called change blindness, the

phenomenon is illustrated in a video (on YouTube) that inspired the duo. Shot in 2007 by British psychologist Richard Wiseman, it ostensibly documents a simple card trick—the backs of the cards in a deck are magically transformed from blue to red. But during the course of the video, Wiseman's shirt, his assistant's shirt, the tablecloth, and the backdrop all change color, too. Most viewers watch the card trick unspool and miss the other alterations.

Attention, it turns out, is like a spotlight. When it's focused on something, we become oblivious to even obvious changes outside its narrow beam. What magicians do, essentially, is misdirect—pivot that spotlight toward the wrong place at the right time.

NOTES

1 Weiner, Edith. "Ten Thinking Technologies." Presentation at The Masters Forum (September 14, 2004). See also her book (with Arnold Brown), *FutureThink: How to Think Clearly in a Time of Change* (Englewood Cliffs, NJ: Prentice Hall, 2005)

2 See Morreall, John, *Humor Works* (Amherst, MA: Human Resource Development Press, 1997)

3 Slywotzky, Adrian. *The Upside: The 7 Strategies for Turning Big Threats into Growth Breakthroughs* (New York: Crown Books, 2007)

4 Slywotzky, Adrian. "The Upside." Presentation at The Masters Forum (November 16, 2007) You can read a summary of this presentation at www.seenewnow.com/summaries/slywotzky.pdf.

5 Pink, Daniel. "A Whole New Mind." Presentation at The Masters Forum (December 6, 2006) You can read a summary of this presentation at www.seenewnow.com/summaries/pink.pdf. See

also his book, *A Whole New Mind: Why Right-Brainers Will Rule the Future* (New York: Riverhead Books, 2006).

6 Lehrer, Jonah. ""Magic and the Brain: Teller Reveals the Neuroscience of Illusion." *Wired* (April 20, 2009) You can read this article at www.wired.com/science/discoveries/magazine/17-05/ff_neuroscienceofmagic. The video mentioned in the excerpt can be seen at www.youtube.com/watch?v=voAntzB7EwE&feature=related.

The Million-Dollar Parrot

Everyone overvalues something.

William Ury, co-author of the great negotiation book *Getting to Yes*,[1] knows as much about negotiation as anyone on the planet. He told this story at The Masters Forum:[2]

> A man is walking down the street. He sees a beautiful parrot in the window of a pet store. He goes inside and asks how much the parrot costs; the owner says "A million dollars."

"A million dollars!"

"Yeah, it's a free country; I can ask what I want for it. Look how beautiful this parrot is! It's worth every penny."

Weeks pass, and the parrot remains in the window. The man stops in regularly to ask whether the owner has come to his senses regarding price. The answer is always the same: a million dollars or no deal.

One day the man sees that the parrot is gone from the window, so he goes in and asks the owner, "Did you sell that parrot?"

"Yes."

"How much did you get for it?"

"A million dollars."

"Somebody really paid a million dollars!?!"

"Well, yes. Actually, I got two chickens, worth five hundred thousand dollars each."

We all have our million-dollar parrots—things we value much more highly than others think we should. It might be an object, like your beloved though slightly tattered tee-shirt from that cool concert you attended ten years ago, or that three-legged chair you bought at a country auction, which you're sure will knock 'em dead on *Antiques Roadshow*. It might be a quality, like your remarkable sense of direction or your extraordinary ability to dominate others at *Monopoly*. It could be an accomplishment.

It could be anything. If you don't have at least two stories of relationships that went awry because you failed to properly acknowledge something that mattered more to the other person than you thought it should (or they failed to do the same toward you), consider yourself lucky.

If you read a corporate statement that brags about the company's unrivalled products, industry-leading technology, or unmatched customer service, keep your eyes open—you may be on the trail of someone's million-dollar parrot.

Maybe if the folks at Bear Stearns hadn't been so enamored of their firm's "reputation for being unusually aggressive even by Wall Street standards,"[3] the whole place might not have melted down around them during the subprime-mortgage crisis. Maybe if Motorola had been less entranced by the thinness of its Razr line of cell phones in 2006, it wouldn't have suffered crushing losses and market-share declines to all-time lows by 2008 as competitors introduced new products and Motorola was stuck with its old ones. "Motorola," the *Wall Street Journal* reported, "put engineers and designers who could have been working on new products on the Razr and its derivatives...'All resources went to feeding the beast,' says a former Motorola designer."[4] Polly want a engineer?

Conversely, Intel's survival today can be traced to the day in 1984 when company president Andrew Grove and CEO Gordon Moore faced up to that company's million-dollar parrot. They had broken away from their previous employer in 1968 to form Intel because of the promise they saw in memory chips. Intel's strategic frame became "Intel means memory."[5] But the memory-chip business declined drastically in the 1970s and 1980s, and Intel was about to face a major crisis. "The company's top executives simply could not believe the growing evidence that they were being outcompeted in a market they had created," explains business historian Richard Tedlow. "Intel was the memory company, period."[6]

Grove asked Moore, "If we got kicked out and the board brought in a new CEO, what do you think he would do?" Moore answered that a new CEO would abandon the production of memory chips and move into microprocessors. Grove suggested, "Why shouldn't you and I walk out that door, come back in, and do it ourselves?"[7] Which they did, sacrificing their million-dollar parrot and saving the company as a result.

Million-dollar parrots pop up in relationships within organizations, too. Your CEO may think her strategy is a lot better than you think it is; you may think your skills at giving positive feedback and recognition are a whole lot better than others think they are; Joe may believe that the sales contacts he's made out on the golf course are worth more than others think they are. In his book *Organizational Diagnosis*, psychologist Harry Levinson warns consultants against acting too quickly to confront a long-standing problem that everybody in an organization recognizes but no one has done anything about—strong, idiosyncratic personal preferences of powerful people, Levinson cautions, probably are at the heart of such an issue.[8]

Here's a concluding tip. Can you imagine that pet shop owner saying or thinking something like this: "Darn it, this parrot is worth a million bucks and I'm not settling for a penny less. It's a matter of principle." Research shows that when people know intuitively that they may be overvaluing something but they're not willing to revise that evaluation, they tend to retreat to "matter of principle" arguments. And, when any issue in a negotiation is defined as a matter of principle, it becomes much more difficult to settle the matter in a mutually-satisfactory way—although two chickens or their equivalents might help.

A Niece Problem to Have

Roger Fisher, co-author of *Getting to Yes,* shared this story at The Masters Forum:[9]

> When I was buying my house, I made my calculation, figured the house was worth this much. The broker came back and said, "This fellow wants more." I said, "I don't think it's worth more." The broker said, "Neither does he. His niece just got married, and she wants him, the uncle, to give her and her husband a big second mortgage on the house so it will stay in the family. She doesn't want it to go out of the family. So, if he sells it for a high enough price, he can justify not giving it to them. He doesn't want the kids to have the house, and he doesn't want to offend the niece—that's why he wants more money."
>
> I say, "So it's not a money problem, it's a niece problem."... I went back to the drawing board, and I repeated my original offer, but I added a beautiful blue-bound legal agreement, lots of ribbons and seals on it, giving the niece a lifetime first refusal on the house, whenever it changed hands. She can match the market price any time the house is sold during her lifetime, so she can buy it back into the family. Once I understood the seller's interest, I could meet it in other ways.

NOTES

1 Ury, William, and Roger Fisher. *Getting to Yes: Negotiating Agreement without Giving In* (Boston: Houghton Mifflin, 1981; New York: Penguin, 1983). The book has sold millions of copies,

and has been translated into 19 languages. (It's a great book not just about negotiation, but also about human relations in general.) Ury's most recent book is *The Power of a Positive No: Save the Deal, Save the Relationship—and Still Say No* (New York: Bantam Books, 2007)

2 Ury, William. "Principled Negotiation." Presentation at The Masters Forum (March 12, 1991). When he told this story, Ury was not using it in the way we have appropriated it for this lens. It illustrated several important points: generally, that the *position* a person might take in a negotiation often is not the same as the person's *interest* or *interests*; it is just one way of satisfying an interest—in this case, it might be said that the pet shop owner wanted to be paid commensurately with the parrot's beauty, but that an offering other than one million dollars cash (the owner's stated position) was not the only way to meet that interest. More specifically, Ury used it to illustrate that people rarely act in isolation in negotiations: in this case, Ury said, "If you think about that for a minute, someone was smart enough to come along and realize that this man needed to be able to say to his constituency that he'd been paid a million dollars for the parrot."

3 Kelly, Kate, Mike Specter and Randall Smith. "The Fall of Bear Stearns: Bear's Final Moment: An Apology and No Lack of Ire." *Wall Street Journal* (May 30, 2008)

4 Rhoads, Christopher, and Li Yuan. "Dropped Call: How Motorola Fell A Giant Step Behind; As It Milked Thin Phone, Rivals Sneaked Ahead On the Next Generation." *Wall Street Journal* (April 27, 2007)

5 See Sull, Donald, *Why Good Companies Go Bad* (Boston: Harvard Business School Press, 2005)

6 Tedlow, Richard. "The Education of Andy Grove." *Fortune* (December 2, 2005)

7 Grove, Andrew. *Only the Paranoid Survive: How to Exploit the Crisis Points That Challenge Every Company* (New York: Doubleday Business, 1999)

8 Levinson, Harry. *Organizational Diagnosis* (Boston: Harvard University Press, 1976). Other observers make similar points. See, for example, books by Manfred Kets de Vries that include *The Leader on the Couch: A Clinical Approach to Changing People and Organizations* (New York: Wiley, 2006) and *Leaders, Fools and Impostors: Essays on the Psychology of Leadership* (iUniverse.com, 2003).

9 Fisher, Roger. "Getting to Yes." Presentation at The Masters Forum. (April 11, 1989)

Image source: © Steir, Barry. See more at www.bocaratongallery.com

SEE NEW NOW

Einstein's Compass

Little things can drive huge breakthroughs.

Albert Einstein's biographer recounts the following:

> The great awakenings that happen in childhood are usually lost to memory. But for Einstein, an experience occurred when he was 4 or 5 that would alter his life and be etched forever in his mind—and in the history of science.
>
> He was sick in bed one day, and his father brought him a

compass. He later recalled being so excited as he examined its mysterious powers that he trembled and grew cold. The fact that the magnetic needle behaved as if influenced by some hidden force field, rather than through the more familiar mechanical method involving touch or contact, produced a sense of wonder that motivated him throughout his life. "I can still remember—or at least I believe I can remember—that this experience made a deep and lasting impression on me," he wrote on one of the many occasions he recounted the incident. "Something deeply hidden had to be behind things."[1]

Writing to a friend, Einstein said, "I am not more gifted than anybody else, I am just more curious than the average person, and I will not give up on a problem until I have found the proper solution."[2]

Curiosity and problem-solving persistence mean a great deal to organizations. Paul Hawken, the idea-filled entrepreneur behind the Smith & Hawken brand, expressed their importance vividly: "Good management is the art of making problems so interesting and their solutions so constructive that everyone wants to get to work and deal with them."[3]

It could be said that quality-improvement programs in general, and continuous improvement approaches in particular, aim to develop that kind of attitude, often with considerable success. As Toyota became the world's largest automobile manufacturer, its president, Katsuaki Watanabe, told interviewers: "There's no genius in our company. We just do whatever we believe is right, trying every day to improve every bit and piece. But when 70 years of very small improvements accumulate, they become a revolution."[4]

Then there's the remarkably energizing program that senior vice president Julie Gilbert initiated at Best Buy, called WOLF, for Women's Leadership Forum. Far more than what you might think of when you see the word "forum," WOLF is an active, engaged, ongoing process that has involved more than 20,000 women employees of Best Buy (and many men) in changing the company's culture, top to bottom.

In this brief summary of WOLF, let's start with the results. Best Buy CEO Brad Anderson credits WOLF with increasing Best Buy's market share among women by more than two percent in its first 18 months—that's worth about $3.6 billion. Turnover among women at Best Buy in areas where there are active WOLF groups was reduced by 5.7 percent in the first year. The savings from the decreased turnover alone have been enough to pay for the whole WOLF program.

WOLF is an extraordinary program, and you would be well served to read more about it.[5] Here's what Gilbert said at The Masters Forum about one of the keys to its success:

> My hypothesis is that for whatever reason, corporations don't want to admit that people are emotional, and we all choose to do first whatever gives us the most energy. My hypothesis is that things would be much better if more organizations looked at their strategy and the first question they asked themselves was "What is it that gives that person energy?" and then they said, "Given the landscape of the strategy we probably need all kinds of skills and talents, so why don't we take that person who loves to do this piece and make that their part in driving the strategy?"[6]

Emotionless command-and-control may feel powerful and straightforward, Gilbert said, but engaging people in the experience and letting them follow their own best energies, while it might take longer, will accomplish much more. That, she said, is how to "transform an organization authentically and organically, so that it's sustainable."[7]

What Hawken, Watanabe, and Gilbert suggest seems so simple, so resonant of Einstein and his compass. And yet so much data suggest that so few companies succeed at truly inspiring curiosity and turning it into improvements. You could have policies like those at 3M and Google, permitting employees to spend significant percentages of their work time on projects that interest them personally. You could adopt a systematic companywide approach like the one recommended in *Creativity, Inc.* by Jeff Mauzy and Richard Harriman, who have each been in the creativity business for more than 25 years.[8]

But to some extent, it's just a matter of mindset, of actually honoring individuals' capacity to wonder about what's around them and contribute to making things better. A compass is a simple, everyday thing; so are most of the processes and interactions that employees observe all the time.

The story of a General Motors automobile assembly plant in Fremont, California is instructive. For years, the place was a virtual disaster. As one writer described it:

> Over the years, GM-Fremont came to be what one manager called "the worst plant in the world." Productivity was among the lowest of any GM plant, quality was abysmal, and drug and alcohol abuse were rampant both on and off the job. Absenteeism was so high that the plant employed 20% more workers than it needed just to ensure an adequate

labor force on any given day.⁹

GM closed the plant, and then reopened it in a joint venture with Toyota called New United Motorcar Manufacturing, Inc., or NUMMI. The same (unionized) workers were rehired: the average age of an assembly-line employee was 41; most had high school educations. Toyota's collaborative work processes were put in place. Here's how that experiment worked out over the course of a few years:

> By the end of 1986, NUMMI's productivity was higher than that of any other GM facility and more than twice that of its predecessor, GM-Fremont. In fact, NUMMI's productivity was nearly as high as [Toyota's] Takaoka plant, even though its workers were, on average, ten years older and much less experienced with the Toyota production system. Quality, as rated by internal GM audits, customer surveys, and *Consumer Reports* was much higher than at any other GM plant and, again, almost as high as Takaoka's.
>
> Equally important, absenteeism has dropped from between 20% and 25% at the old GM-Fremont plant to a steady 3% to 4% at NUMMI; substance abuse is a minimal problem; and participation in the suggestion program has risen steadily from 26% in 1986 to 92% in 1991.¹⁰

Notice those last lines, about participation in the suggestion program. There were no financial or other incentives for that participation above what GM had offered with its own program. Employees participated because, as all the rest of the data show, they were now engaged in ways that they weren't before. As the author wrote, NUMMI was "built on...the logic of learning, a logic that motivates workers and taps their potential contribution to continuous improvement."¹¹

You could try to counteract the tendencies among executives that stifle creative thinking, identified by the great Chris Argyris as prominently including these four values:

> (1) to define in their own terms the purpose of the situation in which they find themselves, (2) to win, (3) to suppress their own and others' feelings, and (4) to emphasize the intellectual and deemphasize the emotional aspects of problems. To satisfy these governing variables, people tend to use unilateral behavioral strategies such as advocating a position and simultaneously controlling others in order to win that position, controlling the tasks to be done, and secretly deciding how much to tell people and how much is to be distorted.[12]

Argyris has shown that even when leaders *want* to encourage creativity, and even when they believe that they *are* encouraging creativity, those four values and the strategies for satisfying them are often at work, dragging down even the best-intentioned.

So if everything else fails, you could try an approach used—according to the ancient historian Herodotus—by Persian decision-makers to make sure they considered the widest range of creative options:

> It is also their general practice to deliberate upon affairs of weight when they are drunk; and then on the morrow, when they are sober, the decision to which they came the night before is put before them by the master of the house in which it was made; and if it is then approved of, they act on it; if not, they set it aside. Sometimes, however, they are sober at their first deliberation, but in this case they always reconsider the matter under the influence of wine.[13]

Well, maybe that's not really something you want to try,

particularly when there are so many simple and effective ways to engage everyone's best talents and greatest curiosity—as long as you are paying attention to what really matters to them.

Teach Your Children Well

Considerable research shows that many of today's most imaginative people had, as Einstein did, a curiosity that they nourished from the time they were quite young.[14] So it might be valuable to heed the words of the great Spanish cellist Pablo Casals, who wrote:

> Each second we live is a new and unique moment of the universe, a moment that will never be again. And what do we teach our children? We teach them that two and two make four, and that Paris is the capital of France. When will we also teach them what they are? We should say to each of them: Do you know what you are? You are a marvel. You are unique. In all the years that have passed, there has never been another child like you. Your legs, your arms, your clever fingers, the way you move. You may become a Shakespeare, a Michelangelo, a Beethoven. You have the capacity for anything. Yes, you are a marvel. And when you grow up, can you then harm another who is, like you, a marvel? You must work, we must all work, to make the world worthy of its children.[15]

NOTES

1 Isaacson, Walter. *Einstein: His Life and Universe.* (New York: Simon & Schuster, 2007). The realizations sparked by the

compass, Einstein said, eventually led him to the theory of relativity. See Updike, John, "The Valiant Swabian: A New Biography of Albert Einstein." *The New Yorker* (April 2, 2007) at www.newyorker.com/arts/critics/books/2007/04/02/070402crbo_books_updike

2 Isaacson, op. cit.

3 Hawken, Paul. *Growing A Business*. (Simon & Schuster, 1988)

4 Stewart, Thomas, and Anand Rama. "Lessons from Toyota's Long Drive." *Harvard Business Review* (July-August, 2007)

5 Our session summary of a three-hour presentation by Gilbert is a very good place to start (see next endnote). See also Fetterman, Mindy. "Best Buy Gets in Touch with Its Feminine Side." *USA Today* (Dec. 20, 2006); and an interview with Gilbert, "Adding their Best to Best Buy," at *In Women We Trust* (May 10, 2008): http://inwomenwetrust.typepad.com/in_women_we_trust/julie_gilbert

6 Gilbert, Julie. "Transformation: How to Get There From Here." Presentation at the Masters Forum (September 11, 2007). You can read a summary of that presentation at www.seenewnow/summaries/gilbert.pdf.

7 Ibid.

8 *Creativity, Inc.: Building An Inventive Organization* (Harvard Business School Press, 2003)

9 Adler, Paul. "Time and Motion Regained." *Harvard Business Review* (January-February, 1993)

10 Ibid.

11 Ibid. One of the authors of the lens you are now reading (Jerry) worked as a consultant at NUMMI in 1989. I taught a

workshop on project management to mixed groups of American and Japanese "team members," which is what everyone who worked at NUMMI, from the top of the organization chart to the bottom, was called. In the first workshop, I was talking about setting project objectives. Knowing that the Toyota approach called for unanimous approval of many things, I suggested a sample objective: "The Employee Handbook must be approved by all team members." Several of the Japanese participants shook their heads. "What's wrong?" I asked. One answered: "You made 'Employee Handbook' the subject of your sentence. We don't do it that way. Team members are always the subject of the sentence. They are what is always most important. The objective should read, 'All team members must approve the Employee Handbook.' " A powerful lesson, for this consultant, about the way values are enacted in organizations.

12 Argyris, Chris, and D. Schon. "Double Loop Learning in Organizations." *Harvard Business Review* (September-October, 1977)

13 Herodotus. *The Histories* (Marincola, John, editor; de Selincourt, Aubery, translator). (New York: Penguin Classics, 2003)

14 See, for example, Holton, Gerald. "On the Role of Themata in Scientific Thought." *Science* (April 25, 1975), in which Holton explores the "nascent moment" at which a young person developed an idea that would guide his or her later scientific interests; and John-Steiner, Vera. *Notebooks of the Mind: Explorations of Thinking*, (University of New Mexico Press, 1984), in which she writes, "Creativity requires a continuity of concern, an intense awareness of one's active inner life combined with sensitivity to the external world... Intensity is

the one universal given in this account of creative thinking; its origins are usually found in childhood"; and Gardner, Howard, *Frames of Mind: The Theory of Multiple Intelligences* (New York: Basic Books, 1993), pages 151-154, where he discusses the impact of childhood experiences on highly accomplished mathematicians and logicians (such as Stanislaw Ulam, who "was fascinated as a young child by the complex patterns in an Oriental rug").

15 Casals, Pablo, and Albert Kahn. *Joys and Sorrows* (Simon & Schuster, 1981)

Image source: ©istockphoto/JLGutierrez

The Itsy Bitsy Spider

Organizational incompetence has a theme song.

Robert Fulghum, whose seven books include *All I Need to Know I Learned in Kindergarten*, is one of the best-selling authors of all time. There are more than 16 million copies of his books in print, published in 27 languages in 103 countries.

When Fulghum received an honorary degree from Syracuse University and delivered its commencement address, he began in a surprising way. Here's how one person described it:

> At first, he didn't say anything. He just stood there, dressed in academic regalia, making silly motions with his hands and fingers. But then the motions became recognizable. For there wasn't a person in the audience (including me) who hadn't seen or made them.
>
> Once the initial motions were complete, Fulghum repeated them. Only this time he burst into song. Whereupon everybody in his audience (including me) began to sing with him.[1]

What Fulghum was gesturing and soon everyone was singing was the childhood song "The Itsy Bitsy Spider."

Saying, "This is the fight song of the human race," and comparing the song's themes to Beethoven's Ninth Symphony, he then told the graduates, "I don't know how many of you have ever looked up a waterspout. It's very dark and very dangerous-looking up there, scary, but there is light showing. The song does not say, 'And the spider said to hell with that and did something else.' Like the spider, we have gone out for hundreds of thousands of years, to go into dangerous places, to find out what's out there, up there."[2]

So you can consider this to be a lens about courage and discovery and perseverance. About, as one writer put it, "a quality of yearning and the potential for fulfillment."[3] Or another: "A reminder that this upward climb is well-nigh universal. People have done it before us. People will do it after us. We encourage it from generation to generation."[4]

Or you could wonder, organizationally, what makes people feel like itsy bitsy spiders, and how much of the stuff coming down that waterspout is really necessary, and how much it is the case that individuals have to keep picking themselves up and climbing up the same spout, or one just like it, over and again. "Somehow," says Stanford Business School professor Jeffrey Pfeffer, "we've gotten in our minds that to succeed in this world is to work yourself to death."[5]

Are there mistakes we keeping making, which we then ask people to go out and overcome? Things we keep doing, in slightly modified forms, that feel like climbing that same old spout? Doing that might make people seem noble, but what does it say about wasted resources and misused energy?

It's going to rain again, for sure. Everyone knows that. To what extent is your organization (or are you) living up to that famous definition of insanity that's often attributed to Einstein: doing the same thing over and over again and expecting different results?

Perseverance and Its Neurotic Manifestations

from "Behind the Medspeak," by Joseph Stirt[6]

Perseveration is a medical term for a brain dysfunction which causes people to persist in a task even though they know rationally that the chosen strategy is doomed and may even be mortally dangerous.

A new analysis suggests that perseveration caused by an earlier head wound is what led German pilot Manfred von Richthofen, World War I's fabled "Red Baron," to chase a British pilot into enemy airspace on April 21, 1918, allowing aircraft and ground fire to cut his Fokker triplane to ribbons and kill him with a single bullet through the chest.

Daniel Orme, a University of Missouri clinical psychologist, said, "He had target fixation and mental rigidity. He flew into a shooting gallery, violating all kinds of rules of flying—rules from the manual that he himself wrote."

NOTES

1 Ritter, William. "On Singing A Baccalaureate Song." at www.fumcbirmingham.org

2 Christian, Nichole. "Commencements." *New York Times* (May 11, 1998)

3 Finley, Michael. "Robert Fulghum: A Finite Gesture Toward Infinite Concerns." at http://mfinley.com/experts/fulghum/Fulghum_Precis.htm. At http://mfinley.com, you can also read many other essays by Finley derived from presentations at The Masters Forum.

4 Ritter. Op. cit. To read how a person who heard Fulghum deliver a sermon about the spider was moved by it in these ways, see http://www.xanga.com/Xander_Schaan/423337521/guilty-as-charged.html.

5 Quoted in Weaver, Jane. "Job Stress, Burnout on the Rise." *MSNBC* (September 1, 2003) at www.msnbc.msn.com/id/3072410

6 Stirt, Joseph. "Behind The Medspeak: Perseveration Brought Down The 'Red Baron.'" (October 8, 2004) at http://www.bookofjoe.com

Bird-Brained Logic

Binary thinking can be okay for animals, but it's generally unwise for humans.

The paleontologist Stephen Jay Gould possessed one of the most inquisitive and acute minds of his generation. A Harvard faculty member, he wrote twenty books about evolution and more than three hundred essays for the lay reader in *Natural History* magazine.

In one of those essays, he wrote:

> When I first went to sea as a petrified urbanite who had never ridden anything larger than a rowboat, an old sailor (and Navy man) told me that I could chart my way through this aqua incognita if I remembered but one simple rule for life and work aboard a ship: If it moves, salute it; if it doesn't move, paint it.
>
> If we analyze why such a statement counts as a joke (albeit a feeble one) in our culture, we must cite the incongruity of placing such a "mindless" model for making human decisions inside a human skull.
>
> After all, the essence of human intelligence is creative flexibility, our skill in grasping new and complex contexts—in short, our ability to make (as we call them) judgments, rather than to act by the dictates of preset rules. Our enlightened sailor, no matter how successful at combating rust or avoiding the brig, is not following a human style of intelligence.
>
> Yet this inflexible model does represent the style of intelligence followed with great success by most other animals. Many birds, for example, do not recognize their own young and act instead by the rule: care for what is inside the nest; ignore what is outside.
>
> This inflexible style of intelligence can be exploited and commandeered to a nefarious purpose by other species. Cuckoos, for example, lay their eggs in the nests of other birds. A cuckoo hatchling, usually larger and more vigorous than the rightful inhabitants, often expels its legitimate nest mates, while their parents follow the rule: ignore them for their inappropriate location, and feed the young cuckoo instead.[1]

The photo at the beginning of this lens shows a reed warbler feeding a much-larger cuckoo chick in the warbler's nest.

The binary thinking that Gould writes about is not uncommon in organizations. In a 2008 Masters Forum presentation, Steve Kerr, who earned renown when he worked alongside Jack Welch to transform General Electric and who then became managing director and chief learning officer at Goldman Sachs, discussed a principal difference between GE before Welch and GE afterward.

He described a program, called Wing-to-Wing, to speed up the repair of the commercial airplane engines that GE built. A faulty engine would be removed from the commercial airplane, shipped to GE's repair facility, fixed, and returned to the customer. Typically, the process required eleven days: seven at GE's facility and four for the engine to travel to and from the airline's hangar. Using Six Sigma strategies, GE reduced its internal repair time from seven days to six. The company celebrated that accomplishment, which it viewed as a one-seventh reduction in turnaround time. "All of our metrics were based on that seven-day frame," Kerr said, "because that's how long we had control of the engine."[2]

He pointed out that for the customer, however, it was only a one-eleventh reduction in the time that the aircraft was unavailable for service. So GE started examining the entire repair system, even those aspects that were outside its direct control. "And it worked," he said. "We could make a difference." For example, customers' own loading docks sometimes wouldn't pass along the information that a repaired engine had arrived for a day or more—so GE started notifying the customers' managers itself.

GE then expanded the Wing-to-Wing program to all of its businesses. Kerr said that GE's thinking before that time had been binary: "Old GE: Customer creates a problem; laugh at the customer—not our fault." The contrast: "New GE: If they had a bad day, we had a bad day. Now that it's part of *our* scorecard, we get mightily interested." From binary thinking—GE on one side and the customer on the other; what's ours is ours, what's the customer's is the customer's—GE embraced the kind of deliberately-chosen mutuality that humans can achieve and binary-thinking animals cannot.

"The affection we got, the customer loyalty we got from this effort, from Wing-to-Wing, we had never seen before. It just was a tremendous tool for loyalty," Kerr said.

Binary thinking has of course been roundly criticized by many modern management theorists. Most executives have heard at least one call to abandon "either/or" viewpoints and to embrace the "and."[3] But knowing what's "right" and what's "wrong," what's "mine" and what's "yours," is a lifetime habit—one that even gets rewarded, often, as evidence of "decisiveness"—that is not so easy to break.

A.G. Lafley revitalized a stumbling Procter & Gamble when he became CEO in 2000. In seven years after he took office, sales grew by double digits and margins reached above 50 percent, while R&D spending declined from 4.8 percent of sales to 3.2 percent. One way he accomplished that was by outsourcing a lot of R&D with the company's pathbreaking "Connect & Develop" program, which invites external innovators to link their discoveries and capabilities with P&G's needs. Over a thousand such partnerships were created in the program's first few years.[4] Lafley said, "We weren't going to win if it was an 'or.' Everybody can do 'or'; everybody can do tradeoffs. But you're not going to win if you're in a tradeoff game."[5]

After decades of research, psychologist Al Siebert reached a similar conclusion concerning personal resilience. It's all about multidimensionality—the capacity to use seemingly opposite behaviors depending on what a situation calls for. As he explained to an interviewer:

> Sometimes in my seminars I distribute what looks like a typical personality-profile questionnaire, with paired items. You know, are you strong-willed or easy-going; trusting or cautious; introverted or extroverted? That kind of thing. I then tell people that if they can readily select one or the other description from those pairs, they're not likely to be very resilient. That's because resilient people are paradoxical—they can do both one behavior and its opposite; they have easy access to a wide range of behaviors.[6]

"Life in companies is only going to get more demanding, and asking people to behave like automatons is asking for dysfunction," Seibert said. So wherever you see binary logic, it may be worthwhile to ask whether it's justified or bird-brained.

A Record-Setting Partnership

The record for the most home runs by a major-league baseball player belongs to Sadaharu Oh, a Japanese player who hit 868 career homers (over 200 more than the next-highest total by a Japanese slugger). In his book, *A Zen Way of Baseball*, Oh explains his hitting philosophy as follows:

> I'm not beating the pitcher. I consider the pitcher my partner in creating the home run.[7]

NOTES

1 Gould, Stephen. "The Guano Ring," in *Hens' Teeth and Horses' Toes: Further Reflections on Natural History* (New York: Norton, 1984). On the internet, you can see photos of "a tiny cuckoo hatchling wickedly hoisting an egg on its back and tossing it over the side [of the nest]." See, for example, Armstrong, Richard, "Cuckoos and Cuckoldry," at *Engines of Our Ingenuity*: www.uh.edu/engines/epi2231.htm.

2 Kerr, Steve. "Crucial Threats and Opportunities in Business Today." Presentation at The Masters Forum (February 12, 2008). You can read a summary of this presentation at www.seenewnow.com/summaries/fuller_and_kerr.pdf.

3 See, for example, Collins, James, *Built to Last: Successful Habits of Visionary Companies* (New York: HarperCollins, 2000); and Martin, Roger, *The Opposable Mind: How Successful Leaders Win Through Integrative Thinking* (Boston: Harvard Business School Press, 2006)

4 See Huston, Larry, and Nabil Sakkab, "Connect and Develop: Inside Procter & Gamble's New Model for Innovation." *Harvard Business Review* (March, 2006)

5 _____. "The Best (& Worst) Managers of the Year: A.G. Lafley." *BusinessWeek* (January 13, 2003)

6 Seibert, Al (interviewed by Gerald de Jaager). "Who Survives? The Battle Belongs to the Versatile and Industrious." Seibert's books include *The Resiliency Advantage* (San Francisco: Berrett-Koehler, 2005) and *The Survivor Personality* (New York: Perigee, 1996).

7 Oh, Sadaharu, and David Falkner. *A Zen Way of Baseball* (New York: Times Books, 1984)

Image: "Reed warbler feeding a Common Cuckoo chick in nest." Olsen, H. Wikimedia Commons.

Shooting David Petraeus

Leaders often learn from going against the grain.

In January of 2007, General David Petraeus was appointed as the commander of all military coalition forces in Iraq. His distinguished career and expertise in counterinsurgency tactics made him the choice of military and governmental leaders to take charge of the new "surge" strategy.

There almost was no General Petraeus. In 1991, when Petraeus was a colonel conducting a live-fire exercise at Fort Campbell, a young soldier, Specialist Terrence Jones, tripped and discharged his M-16 rifle.

Michael Yon, a former Green Beret and an independent journalist, tells what happened:

> The bullet from Spc. Jones' weapon struck Col. Petraeus, slamming through his chest and taking a piece of his back on the way out. Petraeus fell to the ground, bleeding out of his mouth. He nearly died. We could have lost one of the most important and influential military leaders in generations to a mistake, to a professional misstep.[1]

Jones's supervisor was Captain Fred Johnson. Yon observes, "The best that Capt. Johnson and Spc. Jones might have hoped for was a painless end to their military service… Conventional wisdom stipulates that for balance to be restored after accidentally shooting and nearly killing a superior officer, a sacrifice of some magnitude is necessary. A soldier just can't shoot a commander in the chest and walk away. There is no such thing as an 'accidental discharge.' Unplanned bullet launches are called 'negligent discharges.' As in negligent homicide."[2]

Petraeus, however, did not adhere to the conventional wisdom. Captain Johnson, now Lieutenant Colonel Johnson, was promoted early, on Petraeus's say-so. Specialist Jones was sent to Ranger School, which Yon describes as an honor "some young soldiers only dream about."

This could be a lens about giving second chances. But it's worth remembering that Petraeus's willingness to explore and undertake the unconventional is what made him an expert in the unconventional combination of combat and peacemaking that qualified him to lead the "surge" in Iraq. Time will tell how Petraeus's leadership has ultimately affected the course of world events, but it's not too soon to recognize the quality of his contributions.

Leaders and innovative thinkers very often are unconventional. Organizations generally are not very comfortable with the unconventional. Some organizations do a great deal to promote unconventional thinking; many more organizations pay lip-service to it but react to it as though it were a threat rather than an opportunity. Who knows what pressures, explicit and implicit, Petraeus had to deal with as he rewarded the men responsible for his shooting, instead of punishing them as military tradition called on him to do? Who knows how that process reinforced his commitment to trying new ways of doing things, even if those methods ran against longstanding custom? Where might he, or we, be if he hadn't?

Does all that argue for more tolerance in your own organization for the mavericks, the tradition-busters, and even the "failures" who might have learned lessons that others have not? Perhaps so.

Speaking at The Masters Forum, Joseph Fuller, the president of the international consulting firm Monitor Group, reported a story that had been told to him by Ralph Larsen, the former chairman and CEO of Johnson & Johnson:

> Earlier in his career, Larsen was in charge of the launch of Johnson & Johnson disposable diapers.... It was an epic disaster...the biggest write-off in Johnson & Johnson's history.... He walked into his boss's office and said, "I am responsible for this disaster. It was my strategy. It has failed. I am prepared to resign." His boss looked at him and said,

"Why would I fire you, having just paid fifty million dollars to educate you?"[3]

"That story is still told at Johnson & Johnson today," Fuller said.[4]

Petraeus honored the unconventional and the second chance, and he lived those values, which are at the heart of leadership in any learning-based organization. Four years before the shooting incident, in fact, he earned a Ph.D. from Princeton's Woodrow Wilson School for a dissertation in which he studied the American military's mistakes in Vietnam. Perhaps expecting that one day the armed forces would receive a "second chance" to enact lessons learned in that earlier conflict, he wrote:

> Vietnam cost the military dearly. It left America's military leaders confounded, dismayed, and discouraged. Even worse, it devastated the armed forces, robbing them of dignity, money, and qualified people for a decade.... While the psychic scars of the war may be deepest among the Army and Marine Corps leadership, however, the senior leaders of all the services share a similar reaction to Vietnam. There is no desire among any of them to repeat the experience that provided the material for such descriptively titled books as: "Defeated: Inside America's Military Machine"; "Self Destruction: the Disintegration and Decay of the United States Army During the Vietnam Era"; and "Crisis in Command: Mismanagement in the United States Army."[5]

The columnist Peggy Noonan tells of Petraeus in 2007, gathering together troops under his command in Iraq at a sweltering desert compound and telling them what had happened to him in 1991. Asked why he related the story, Petraeus said, "The point was to tell them, 'Listen, if you're not perfect right now you can grow, you can make mistakes, people are forgiving, you'll grow.' "[6]

A second chance can be a good thing, for individuals and organizations. By giving second chances to some individuals, David Petraeus may have changed not only their lives, but the way the Army thinks about "negligent discharges." By studying the history of Vietnam, Petraeus may have created two second chances: one to overcome a painful legacy from the past, and one to rectify the shortcomings of the military's initial approach in Iraq. A 700-page study conducted by the Army of its Iraq strategy, released in 2008, observed, "The Army, as the service primarily responsible for ground operations, should have insisted on better Phase IV [post-combat] planning and preparations through its voice on the Joint Chiefs of Staff. The military means employed were sufficient to destroy the Saddam regime; they were not sufficient to replace it with the type of nation-state the United States wished to see in its place."[7]

The study's title is *On Point II: Transition to the New Campaign*, and the Army says, "At the core of *On Point II* is the dramatic story of how after May 2003, the US Army reinvented itself by transforming into an organization capable of conducting a broad array of diverse and complex 'Full Spectrum' operations." Without the innovative spirit and culture-bucking experience of David Petraeus, honed in thought and in deed, would such a transformation even have been possible?

The Twice-Born Personality

from "Managers and Leaders: Are They Different?" by Abraham Zaleznik[8]

> ...William James describes two types of personalities, "once-born" and "twice-born." People of the former personality type are those for whom adjustments to life have been straightforward and whose lives have been more or less a peaceful flow since birth. Twice-borns, on the other hand, have not had an easy time of it. Their lives are marked by a continual struggle to attain some sense of order. Unlike once-borns, they can not take things for granted. According to James, these personalities have equally different worldviews. For a once-born personality, the sense of self as a guide to conduct and attitude derives from a feeling of being at home and in harmony with one's environment. For a twice-born, the sense of self derives from a feeling of profound separateness.
>
> A sense of belonging or of being separate has practical significance for the kinds of investments managers and leaders make in their careers. Managers see themselves as conservators and regulators of an existing order of affairs with which they personally identify and from which they gain rewards. A manager's sense of self-worth is enhanced by perpetuating and strengthening existing institutions....
>
> Leaders tend to be twice-born personalities, people who feel separate from their environment. They may work in organizations, but they never belong to them. Their sense of who they are does not depend on memberships, work roles, or other social indicators of identity. And that perception of

identity may form the theoretical basis for explaining why certain individuals seek opportunities for change.

NOTES

1 Yon, Michael. "Dispatches from Iraq: Second Chances." (July 9, 2007) at *FoxNews*: www.foxnews.com/story/0,2933,288704,00.html

2 Ibid.

3 Fuller, Joseph. "Crucial Threats and Opportunities in Business Today." Presentation at The Masters Forum (February 12, 2008). You can read a summary of this presentation at www.seenewnow.com/summaries/fuller_and_kerr.pdf

4 For some additional thoughts about this story and its implications, positive and perhaps not so positive, see the lens "The Gorilla in the Midst" at www.seenewnow.com.

5 Dry, Rachel. "Petraeus on Vietnam's Legacy." *Washington Post* (January 14, 2007)

6 Noonan, Peggy. "Get It Done." *Wall Street Journal* (August 10, 2007)

7 Wright, Donald, Timothy Reese, and others. *On Point II: Transition to the New Campaign* (Washington, D.C.: US Government Printing Office, 2008)

8 Zaleznik, Abraham. "Managers and Leaders: Are They Different?" (HBR Classics) *Harvard Business Review* (March-April, 1992)

Image source: "Gen. David Petraeus." © Burke, Lauren. See more at http://wdcpix.com

SEE NEW NOW

The Mile Run

Some tests measure what doesn't matter and miss what does.

Earl Campbell was an astonishingly good football player, very strong and very fast. He won the Heisman Trophy, awarded to the nation's best college football player. There is a nine-foot-high statue of him outside the University of Texas football stadium. ESPN has rated him as the twelfth-best college football player of all time.

In his first year of professional football, he won honors as both Rookie of the Year and as Most Valuable Player. He went on to lead the league in rushing yardage the next three years and garner many awards. After his career ended, he was voted into the Hall of Fame.

Campbell played most of his NFL career for the Houston Oilers, where his head coach was Andrew "Bum" Phillips, who was known for his folksy communication style. Phillips once remarked, "Earl Campbell may not be in a class by himself, but whatever class he's in, it wouldn't take long to call the roll."[1]

One year the Oilers' trainer instituted a practice very common throughout sports at all levels: he required all players to run a mile within a designated time. Campbell, whose thighs were thirty-five inches around and who carried about 240 pounds on a five-foot-ten-inch frame, was not built for distance running. Although he was determined, he never could complete the run on time.

Reporters came to Phillips demanding to know what he was going to do about his star player who could not fulfill one of the team's requirements. "Well, if it's fourth down and a mile to go," Phillips answered them, "I guess we'll have to give the ball to someone else."[2]

Like the mile-run test that measured nothing important about Earl Campbell's abilities or his heart, many organizations apply explicit or implicit tests and rules that prevent individuals from contributing the best they have to offer. Rooting out those very kinds of unproductive rules was the aim of the first major program that Jack

Welch initiated at General Electric. It was called the "Work-Out" program; its goal, Welch wrote, was to put an end to "wrestling with the boundaries, the absurdities that grow in large organizations." "We're all familiar with those absurdities," Welch added, "too many approvals, duplication, pomposity, waste."[3] In GE's 1997 *Annual Report*, Welch proudly announced: "After a decade of Work-Out, most of the old bureaucracy and the boundaries among us have been demolished... [A]t GE today, finding the better way, the best idea, from whomever will share it with us, has become our central focus."[4]

Today, Wikipedia provides a notable example of eliminating unnecessary impediments and letting people contribute what they can. As a writer opined regarding Wikipedia's founder Jimmy Wales: "Wales's most radical contribution may be not to have made information free but to have invented a system that does not favor the Ph.D. over the well-read fifteen-year-old."[5] Wales has said: "To me, the key thing is getting it right. I don't care if they're a high-school kid or a Harvard professor."[6]

The best and most effective diversity programs seek to eradicate counterproductive tests, rules, and individual practices: not just the race- or gender-based criteria that have excluded so many from full participation in our society's institutions, but also the other hurdles that we all create, often unwittingly, that keep us from using the best inputs and abilities of others.

Some rules are good for some things and not for others. Writing in *Harvard Business Review* in 2008, innovation guru Clayton Christensen said of certain core financial tools—including the use of discounted cash flows and net present value calculations, and an emphasis on earnings-per-share analyses—"the way they are commonly wielded in evaluating investments creates a systematic bias against innovation."[7]

Just as distance running might have tested something valuable about Earl Campbell's teammates but not about Campbell himself, those financial screens can be useful in some applications, but they're counterproductive in others.

The same may be true of tests we all create in our own lives that rule out some people, some ideas, and some experiences for reasons that don't hold up under examination. They're not "reasons" at all, often; they're just habits of seeing and thinking that have solidified into tests and rules.

The story is told of a young girl at school whose teacher asked, "What color are apples?" "Red!" answered one student. "Very good," said the teacher. "Green!" answered another, also receiving a positive response from the teacher. "Yellow!" "Yes. Some apples are golden yellow." "White," said the young girl. "White?" answered the teacher. "Why, no, I don't believe I've ever seen a white apple." "Yes, they are white," the girl insisted. "No," said the teacher. "They can be red, or green, or yellow, but not white."

"Look inside," said the girl.

When our rules consider only what's on the surface and ignore what's underneath, we're not getting the best out of them.

Brilliant Guy, No Degree

from Steve Jobs' 2005 Stanford University Commencement Address:[8]

> I am honored to be with you today at your commencement from one of the finest universities in the world. I never

graduated from college. Truth be told, this is the closest I've ever gotten to a college graduation... I naively chose a college that was almost as expensive as Stanford, and all of my working-class parents' savings were being spent on my college tuition. After six months, I couldn't see the value in it. I had no idea what I wanted to do with my life and no idea how college was going to help me figure it out. And here I was spending all of the money my parents had saved their entire life. So I decided to drop out.... [L]ooking back, it was one of the best decisions I ever made. The minute I dropped out I could stop taking the required classes that didn't interest me, and begin dropping in on the ones that looked interesting.

NOTES

1 Kirschenbaum, Jerry, ed. "They Said It." *Sports Illustrated* (November 12, 1979)

2 This quote is reported in different ways. See, for example, MacMahon, Tim, "Wade Made Us Wait." *Dallas Morning News SportsDay* (August 7, 2007)

3 Slater, Robert. *Jack Welch and the GE Way* (New York: McGraw-Hill, 1998)

4 Welch, John, Paolo Fresco, and others. "Letter to Our Share Owners and Employees." *General Electric Company 1997 Annual Report*

5 Schiff, Stacy. "Know It All." *The New Yorker* (July 31, 2006) at www.newyorker.com/archive/2006/07/31/060731fa_fact

6 Ibid.

7 Christensen, Clayton, Stephen Kaufman, and Willy Shih. "Inno-

vation Killers: How Financial Tools Destroy Your Capacity to Do New Things." *Harvard Business Review* (January, 2008)

8 _____. " 'You've Got to Find What You Love,' Jobs Says." *Stanford Report* (June 14, 2005) at http://news-service.stanford.edu/news/2005/june15/jobs-061505.html

Abwoon D'bwashmaya

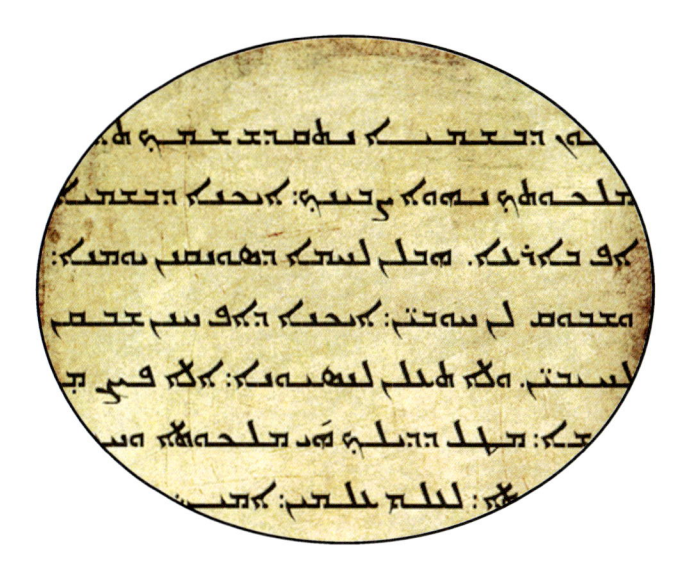

How things are is not the only way they could be.

The "Lord's Prayer" is a central aspect of worship in many Christian churches. It begins with the words *Abwoon d'bwashmaya*.

Or, at least, it *began* with those words. *Abwoon d'bwashmaya* is the Aramaic pronunciation of the words that the King James Bible renders as "Our Father which art in heaven."[1] Jesus spoke in Aramaic.[2] The words of Jesus in the King James Bible are English translations of Latin and Greek translations of his original Aramaic words. Aramaic was a very different language than English (or Greek or Latin): much less precise, much more mystical, much more rooted in the physical world. One word may have many different meanings. To see one scholar's take on how *Abwoon d'bwashmaya* might be translated, see note 3.

This is just our way of suggesting the following lens: You can become so used to things as you know them that it might not occur to you that they could be different than they are.[4]

Lots of great product ideas have come from seeing everyday things in new ways. People drank lots of mundane coffee until Starbucks came along; they dragged and toted heavy suitcases until someone thought to put wheels on them;[5] and they accepted more fat than they wanted in their hamburgers until George Foreman introduced his grill.[6]

Here's another example, one that could be a lens all by itself. Call it "The Factory Gates." In the 1860s, New England textile mills began harnessing the power of steam engines to drive mass-production looms. To make the most of that technology, it was necessary to insure reliable attendance by the mill workers, so the owners of one mill posted a new set of rules: all weavers were to enter the plant at the same time, after which the gates would be locked until the end of the workday.

Deeply offended by what they called a "system of slavery," the weavers—who until then had worked whatever hours they pleased—went on strike. The rules were withdrawn, and it was not until several years later that they could be successfully reintroduced. Few people today question an employer's right to establish standardized working hours. What at first seems novel, even revolutionary, becomes routinized into the fabric of daily worklife and breeds other norms, which then also become accepted as a standard way of doing things.[7]

You can be so close to something for so long—in business, that might be not just a product or service but a customary way of doing things; in your relationships, it might be a pattern or habit developed over a long time—that you risk losing the fuller, richer life that once lay behind—and within—it. You think you know it, but maybe you don't. You think it's the way things have to be, but maybe it isn't.

The Challenges of Seeing New Now

from *Tell Me a Story* by Roger Schank[8]

In a sense, many situations in life have the people who participate in them seemingly reading their roles in a kind of play. The more scripts you know, the more situations will exist in which you feel comfortable and capable of playing your role effectively. But the more scripts you know, the more situations you will fail to wonder about, be confused by, and have to figure out on your own.

NOTES

1 Aramaic pronunciations are difficult to render, so many phrases similar to *Abwoon d'bwashmaya* can be found, including *Avvon d-bish-maiya* and *Abwun d'bwaschmaja*. You can hear the words spoken and sung at www.savae.org/realaudioclips/abwoon.clip2.mp3, and in many youtube clips, for example at

www.youtube.com/watch?v=vPE6Rv7RgW0

2 This is the widely accepted, though unprovable view. Some assert that Jesus spoke Hebrew. Among the evidence that Jesus spoke Aramaic are several Bible passages in which Jesus's Aramaic words are translated by a Gospel writer. For example, Mark 15:34: "And at the ninth hour Jesus cried with a loud voice, saying, *Eloi, Eloi, lama sabachthani?* which is, being interpreted, My God, my God, why hast thou forsaken me?"

3 In part because Aramaic is so complex, scholars differ widely over how the Lord's Prayer might be translated. Here is one discussion of the first word, *Abwoon* ("Our Father" in the King James version):

A: The Absolute, the Only Being, the pure Oneness and Unity, Divine Parent, Source of all Power and Stability, or Foundation. (Echoing the ancient sound Al—the Sacred Sound—and the Aramaic word "Alaha" literally, "the Oneness.")

BW: A Birthing, a Creation, a Flow of Blessing, as if from the "interior" of this Oneness to us.

OO: The Breath or Spirit that carries this flow of blessing, echoing the sound of breathing and including all the magnificent forces we now call magnetism, wind, electricity, and more. This sound is linked to the Aramaic phrase "Rukha d'qoodsha"—which was later translated as "Holy Spirit."

N: The vibration of this creative breath from Oneness as it touches and interpenetrates form. There must be a substance that this force touches, moves and changes. This sound echoes the Earth Mother.

As a complex sound, this word encompasses the Creator, the Created, and Creation, or the Knower, the Known, and the process of Knowing.

See Douglas-Glotz, Neil, *Prayers of the Cosmos: Meditations on the Aramaic Words of Jesus* (San Francisco: HarperSanFrancisco, 1990).

4 In this regard, it might be worth mentioning that in a 2003 survey, Jesus was ranked thirteenth, in a tie with Bill Clinton, by people who were asked to name the greatest Americans of all time. Source: "Harper's Index." *Harper's* (March, 2003)

5 According to the *New York Times*, the first suitcase on wheels was produced in 1972. It was derisively rejected when its inventor first showed it to a buyer at Macy's. As of the year 2000, the date of the *Times* story, the inventor was still earning royalties from his creation. See Kilgannon, Corey, "From Suitcases on Wheels to Tear-Free Onion Slicers." *New York Times* (August 6, 2000).

6 More than 100 million George Foreman grills have been sold, making it the best-selling kitchen appliance in history.

7 See Zuboff, Shoshana, "New Worlds of Computer-Mediated Work." *Harvard Business Review* (September-October, 1982). See also her book, *In the Age of the Smart Machine: The Future of Work and Power* (New York: Basic Books, 1989).

8 Schank, Roger. *Tell Me a Story: Narrative and Intelligence.* (Evanston, IL: Northwestern University Press, 1995)

Image: "The Lord's Prayer in Aramaic." Dangelo, 2008

SEE NEW NOW

The Insect-Size Buffalo

Too much close-in thinking can warp your sense of perspective.

In the 1950s, the anthropologist Colin Turnbull lived for several years with the BaMbuti people in the dense Ituri forest of Africa, which had only a few small clearings. One day Turnbull brought a young BaMbuti man, Kenge, with him to an open plain. Here's what happened next:

> Kenge looked over the plains and down to where a herd of about a hundred buffalo were grazing some miles away. He asked me what kind of insects they were, and I told him they were buffalo, twice as big as the forest buffalo known to him. He laughed loudly and told me not to tell such stupid

stories, and asked me again what kind of insects they were. He then talked to himself, for want of more intelligent company, and tried to liken the buffalo to the various beetles and ants with which he was familiar.

He was still doing this when we got into the car and drove down to where the animals were grazing. He watched them getting larger and larger, and though he was as courageous as any Pygmy, he moved over and sat close to me and muttered that it was witchcraft. Finally when he realized that they were real buffalo he was no longer afraid, but what puzzled him still was why they had been so small, and whether they *really* had been small and had suddenly grown larger, or whether it had been some kind of trickery.

As we came over the crest of the last low hill, Lake Edward stretched out into the distance beyond, losing itself in a hazy horizon. Kenge had never seen any expanse of water wider than the Ituri river, a few hundred yards across. This was another new experience difficult for him to comprehend. He again had the same difficulty of believing that a fishing boat a couple of miles out contained several human beings. "But, it's just a piece of wood," he protested. I reminded him of the buffalo, and he nodded unbelievingly.[1]

Because Kenge lived in a closed-in forest and had no experience of seeing distant objects, he had no sense of perspective. Brain science is showing that the same phenomenon occurs in relationship to thinking strategically. Best-selling author Robert Cooper, for example, explains that there's a part of our brains that specializes in helping us think imaginatively about the future, resisting our instinct to involve ourselves in nothing but the minutia of day-to-day survival, which Cooper describes as "shoetop gazing." That strategic-thinking brain part, Cooper says, is like a muscle—when it's not exercised it atrophies. Here are his chilling words about what happens next: "You can permanently lose the capacity to truly envision a future for yourself in any but the most wishful and fantastical ways: one day that capacity just vanishes, along with your ability to realistically plot a way from where you are now to someplace you want to be in the future."[2]

There's not much point, organizationally or personally, in focusing only on the closed-in space of today's to-do list or the current quarter's performance, while at the same time hoping that next year or five years from now you will achieve some larger open-space dream. Perhaps it's no wonder that so many people in organizations, when hearing the latest "vision statement" that their management has concocted at an expensive offsite retreat, can only "laugh loudly," like Kenge, and request not to be told such "stupid stories."

You can look at the place of data in organizational life in a similar way. There's so much of it—but without perspective, it is impossible to tell which has the heft of a buffalo and which is as insubstantial as an insect. Speaking at The Masters Forum in 2008, Joseph Fuller, CEO of the Monitor consulting organization, asserted, "There is tidal wave of data hitting companies, which you are responsible for knowing about if you're a decision-maker. The problem is that there's so much of it that no one is going to actually sort through all that stuff and know what to make of it. So it becomes incredibly important to actually know what you're looking for."[3]

Fuller recommended two ways to separate the gnats from the

gnus. First, ask, "If I knew something different about the decision I am about to make, would it cause me to make a different choice? What would I need to know to choose option A or option B? What data would have to be different?"

Second, Fuller said, do not assume that your perspective is correct. When dealing with others,

> Rather than going at them with your advocacy—"I have analyzed this and this is the right answer"—go at them with your inquiry: "What do you need to know to feel comfortable about this decision? What are the questions you have about our strategy or our approach that, if you could get more information about it, would make you feel more comfortable?"

So much of organizational life is a matter of gaining the perspective from which to differentiate the insects from the buffalo.

In our personal and organizational lives, it can be helpful to know that some psychological systems categorize people as either maximizers or minimizers. Maximizers act as though everything's a big deal; to minimizers, practically nothing is. Minimizers tend to live in closed-in space: they turn feelings inward rather than expressing them outwardly; they don't disclose much about themselves; they tend to deny their needs. They act as though everything's the size of an insect, in contrast to maximizers, who have opposite characteristics and for whom everything's a buffalo. At least one respected authority has said that couples often consist of a minimizer and a maximizer.[4]

(By the way, when you read about "buffalo" in Turnbull's account at the beginning of this lens, did you think of an American buffalo, or bison? If so, did that interfere with your concentration? Somewhere in the back of your mind were you asking something like, "Are there *buffalo* in *Africa*?" Well, of course there are—they're shown in the photo at the beginning of this lens—but it probably would have been easier for you to fluidly read the story if Kenge had been seeing giraffes or gazelles. For some information about how our brains work as we read and as we think, and how we integrate or don't integrate new information, see the lens in this book titled "The Garden Path.")

The Ground and the Horizon

from "Perceiving Perception," by Jim Smith[5]

Suppose it was your job to evaluate candidates applying to become fighter pilots. What do you imagine it takes to make a good fighter pilot? Nerves of steel? Lightning reflexes? Exceptional bravery? Just exactly what attributes would you look for? Answering that question was a matter of real significance to the Air Force during World War II... [M]ilitary officials turned to psychologists to help them explore a number of human dynamics. One of the psychologists engaged in this research—a young Cornell University professor named James J. Gibson—was something of a revolutionary. It was not the candidates' emotional make-up that piqued his interest. It was their visual acuity.

When it came to flying a fighter plane, Gibson knew, the ability to maneuver the plane decisively, to make split-second decisions, could mean the difference between life and death. As a tool for picking candidates most likely to succeed, standard vision tests were useless... [W]hat was really important, Gibson realized, was not so much 20/20 vision as the capacity to quickly process information about spatial relationships and what actually goes into that skill. He was particularly interested in the all-too-frequent phenomenon of claustrophobia and disorientation that overtook pilots when they flew into cloudbanks. The ground and the horizon, he soon understood, were critically important. Indeed, they were the essential construct against which pilots maneuvered their aircraft.

NOTES

1 Turnbull, Colin. "Some Observations Regarding the Experiences and Behavior of the BaMbuti Pygmies." *American Journal of Psychology* (1961). Turnbull's book, *The Forest People*, became very popular after its publication in 1961.

2 Cooper, Robert. *Get Out Of Your Own Way: The 5 Keys to Surpassing Everyone's Expectations* (New York: Crown Books, 2006)

3 Fuller, Joseph. "Crucial Threats and Opportunities in Business Today." Presentation at The Masters Forum (February 12, 2008). You can read a summary of this presentation at www.seenewnow.com/summaries/fuller_and_kerr.pdf.

4 See, for example, Hendrix, Harville, *Getting the Love You Want: A Guide for Couples (Twentieth Anniversary Edition)* (New York: Holt, 2007)

5 Smith, Jim. "Perceiving Perception: Professor William Mace and the World of Ecological Psychology." *Trinity Reporter* (Fall, 2003)

Image source: "Looming Storm." © Dunham, Greg.

The Hedgehog and the Fox

An ancient classification scheme captures a persistent dilemma.

In the preface to his 1983 book *Power In and Around Organizations*, Henry Mintzberg explained how that book differed from his previous ones: "[M]y first two books...were hedgehog books. Each knew one big thing.... This third book...is a fox book. It knows many things."[1]

Mintzberg, who might be the most innovative and imaginative

business theorist of our time, acknowledges in the preface that he didn't originate that fox-and-hedgehog categorization scheme, which was first formulated around the seventh century BCE. In 1953, the eminent British philosopher Sir Isaiah Berlin borrowed it to create what he considered a very valuable lens. He wrote:

> There is a line among the fragments of the Greek poet Archilochus which says: "The fox knows many things, but the hedgehog knows one big thing".... [T]aken figuratively, the words can be made to yield a sense in which they mark one of the deepest differences which divide writers and thinkers, and, it may be, human beings in general. For there exists a great chasm between those, on one side, who relate everything to a single central vision, one system less or more coherent or articulate, in terms of which they understand, think and feel—a single, universal, organizing principle in terms of which alone all that they are and say has significance—and, on the other side, those who pursue many ends, often unrelated and even contradictory, connected, if at all, only in some de facto way, for some psychological or physiological cause, related by no moral or aesthetic principle... The first kind of intellectual and artistic personality belongs to the hedgehogs, the second to the foxes.[2]

Berlin went on to assign writers and philosophers to those categories, placing Shakespeare and Goethe among the foxes, for example, and Dante and Dostoevsky among the hedgehogs.

More currently, observers have generally agreed regarding recent U.S. Presidents that Ronald Reagan was a hedgehog, while Bill Clinton was a fox.[3] (The famous sign posted in Clinton's campaign headquarters—"It's the economy, stupid"—can be seen as a reminder to the foxy Clinton to behave more like a hedgehog on the campaign trail.) As for the more recent presidents, we'll let you decide about them on your own.[4]

Even though caution is advised when categorizing anyone, or anything, too decisively (a wise person once observed, "There are two kinds of people in the world: those who divide the world into two kinds of people and those who don't"[5]), the distinction between foxes and hedgehogs provides a way of talking and thinking about very important differences. In fact, it might be said that the metaphor derives some its power from the fact that it represents a challenge that all people and all organizations face: freedom versus order. As they are depicted in the metaphor's imagery, the rambunctious and impetuous fox discovers new things in its free wanderings but invites risk and danger, while the stolid and incurious hedgehog is protected by its prickly self-containment.

For a very long time, most business theorists conceived of organizations as being hedgehoglike: setting unitary goals, organizing in lockstep to meet those goals, using rewards and punishments to keep people in line, and largely protected from intrusions from the outside world. Even though this model has been challenged by the realities of globalization, human motivation, and the dynamics of a truly competitive marketplace, among other things, it still has a strong hold as the mental model that many leaders carry with them. It helps explain, for instance, why so many managers still practice the leadership method known as "command and control," even as that method has been decried as ineffectual by virtually every thoughtful leadership theorist for the past three decades.

Many business practices have both foxlike and hedgehoglike applications. Strategic planning as it has historically been practiced, with an essentially unitary target, is hedgehoggy; scenario planning is foxier. One-size-fits-all reward systems flow from a hedgehog concept of what motivates people, while tailored or cafeteria-style programs are foxier. Approaches to innovation that rely on new elaborations of existing products are hedgehoglike; ones that seek flurries of ideas for new businesses are foxier.

Jim Collins certified hedgehogginess as a core attribute of organizational greatness in his best-seller *Good to Great*, where he compared companies that elevated themselves from consistent good performance to sustained great performance against other companies that remained good but never became great. Here's a major conclusion Collins reached:

> Those who built the good-to-great companies were, to one degree or another, hedgehogs. They used their hedgehog nature to drive toward what we came to call a Hedgehog Concept for their companies. Those who led the comparison companies tended to be foxes, never gaining the clarifying advantage of a Hedgehog Concept, being instead scattered, diffused, and inconsistent.[6]

Collins's analyses are always deep, robust, and persuasive. It is not to doubt him to also imagine—or, for most people, to recall—leaders whose "hedgehog concept" blinds them to opportunities or insights that less singularly-focused individuals might have embraced.

Substantial research shows that hedgehog individuals are not particularly good at anticipating the future or adjusting to current developments. In a large, long-term study, a scholar analyzed the accuracy of 82,361 political and economic predictions made by 284 acknowledged experts. Before performing the analysis, he and several others had classified each of the experts as either a hedgehog or a fox.[7] While in general the experts had little success at forecasting, the author reported:

> Low scorers look like hedgehogs: thinkers who "know one big thing," aggressively extend the explanatory reach of that one big thing into new domains, display bristly impatience with those who "do not get it," and express considerable confidence that they are already pretty proficient forecasters, at least in the long term. High scorers look like foxes: thinkers who know many small things (tricks of their trade), are skeptical of grand schemes, see explanation and prediction not as deductive exercises but rather as exercises in flexible "ad hocery" that require stitching together diverse sources of information, and are rather diffident about their own forecasting prowess.[8]

Organizations and leaders struggle regularly to find and sustain a proper balance between the advantages and disadvantages of a more orderly, hedgehog approach and a freer, fox approach. Karl Weick has written at length about "sensemaking" as a crucial skill in today's fluid business world. By that term he means actively engaging employees in sorting and sifting information to arrive at tentative understandings and intentions as bases for moving forward, rather than simply interpreting data on the basis of a preexisting model of how things are and how they should be. As one writer summarized Weick's view, "[S]ocial reality is most properly thought of as an ongoing stream of interconnected processes, in most cases without clear beginnings or ends."[9]

As the quote from Collins above indicates, the "hedgehog concepts" that Collins observed were the products of executives' "hedgehog nature." Fox executives might prefer sensemaking as a strategic process. Many examples throughout this book illustrate ways that leaders address hedgehog/fox freedom/order issues: Procter & Gamble reaching outside its orderly corporate boundaries to partner with innovators (see the "Bird-Brained Logic" lens); Intel's top executives deciding to abandon what could be called their "hedgehog concept" ("The Million-Dollar Parrot"); the progression suggested by Larry Greiner's conception of organizational evolution and revolution, where the crises forecast by Greiner tend to be reactions to either too much freedom or too much order ("The Bolero Challenge"); the tension between monolithic rules and individualistic perspectives in "The Mile Run."

Google's manager of open source programming, Chris DiBona, conducted an interesting experiment (without knowing it would turn out to be an experiment) concerning the relative benefits of freedom and control. Employing over 800 students to perform programming work during the summer in Google's "Summer of Code" program, he left the students to work with very little supervision, and, for most of them, no face-to-face supervision at all. The students' productivity was startling—by some measures they were, according to DiBona, "anywhere between 5 and 40 times as productive as your 'average' employed programmer."[10]

That outcome led DiBona to ask deep questions about freedom and control and to reach a tentative conclusion. He writes:

> [I]s the tradeoff for silly high productivity that I have to run my projects the way we run the Summer of Code? Maybe. Can I keep my hands off and let things run their course? Is the team strong enough to act as this kind of mentoring to

each other? I now think the answer is that yes, they can run each other better than I can run them. So let's see what letting go looks like.[11]

Some thoughtful writers see in today's broader culture "a general predisposition to favor the way of the fox,"[12] whereas others notice a valuing of the concentrated hedgehog over the dissipated fox. Here's one story that speaks to the latter view:

> "You care for nothing but shooting, dogs, and rat-catching," Charles Darwin recalled his father once telling him, "and you will be a disgrace to yourself and all your family." It was an inauspicious beginning for one of history's greatest scientists...
>
> Despite misgivings about his son's lack of direction, Robert Darwin consented to let Charles set sail aboard the *Beagle* before returning to England to become, as he planned, a country gentleman and parson. (Charles Darwin halfway succeeded—he remained a country gentleman the rest of his days.) Darwin considered the voyage the defining experience of his life, and he was right—it provided him with the evidence that would forever change biology.[13]

Sometimes it's all going to be about balance, and sometimes it's about discovering your inner hedgehog or fox. The core dichotomy may seem simplistic, but it provides a valuable tool for understanding, acting, and progressing.

Distinctions and Their Perils

from *Making Sense of the Organization*, by Karl Weick[14]

Richard Hackman and I were exchanging penciled sketches

at a meeting of social psychologists to help pass the time more quickly. One of Hackman's drawings shows two gravestones, one for each of us. On his stone is the epitaph, "He saved the world," and on mine is written, "He understood the world," and at the bottom is written, "And they both were kidding themselves."

NOTES

1 Mintzberg, Henry. *Power in and Around Organizations* (Englewood Cliffs, NJ: Prentice-Hall, 1983)

2 Berlin, Isaiah. *The Hedgehog and the Fox: An Essay on Tolstoy's View of History* (New York: Simon & Schuster, 1953)

3 See, for example, Krauthammer, Charles, "Clinton Writ Small," *Washington Post* (June 25, 2004); and Stengel, Richard, "When Foxes Pose as Hedgehogs," *Time* (October 7, 1996).

4 For one (partisan) commentator's categorization of twentieth-century presidents, see Barnett, Thomas, "Enough of the Hedgehog" (January 6, 2007) at www.thomaspmbarnett.com/weblog/2007/01/this_weeks_column_2.html.

5 This comment is often attributed to the author Robert Benchley, and is sometimes referred to as Benchley's Law of Distinction.

6 Collins, James. *Good to Great: Why Some Companies Make the Leap and Others Don't* (New York: HarperBusiness, 2001). For much more on this subject, see Collins's website, www.jimcollins.com.

7 To read a summary of how these classifications were reached, see "The Situation of Prognostication" at http://thesituationist.wordpress.com/category/book

8 Tetlock, Philip. *Expert Political Judgment: How Good Is It? How*

Can We Know? (Princeton, NJ: Princeton University Press, 2005). An extensive discussion of the book is at Menand, Louis, "Everybody's An Expert," *The New Yorker* (December 5, 2005), which can be read at www.newyorker.com/archive/2005/12/05/051205crbo_books1?currentPage=all.

9 Martin, Maximillian. *Globalization, Macroeconomic Stabilization, and the Construction of Social Reality* (Berlin: Lit Verlag, 2005)

10 DiBona, Chris. "Oversight and Programmer Productivity." *Edge World Question Center* at www.edge.org/q2008/q08_15.html.

11 Ibid.

12 Lieberson, Jonathon. "The Hedgehog and the Fox." *New York Review of Books* (Letter: September 25, 1980). This letter also contains an interesting perspective on the original meaning of the phrase "hedgehog and fox" (www.nybooks.com/articles/7297).

13 Scott, Michon. "Charles Darwin," at *Strange Science: The Rocky Road to Modern Paleontology and Biology* (November 3, 2007): www.strangescience.net/darwin.htm

14 Weick, Karl. *Making Sense of the Organization* (New York: Wiley-Blackwell, 2000)

SEE NEW NOW

The Puddle

Being comfortable can be the first step toward being gone.

Douglas Adams charmed many millions of people with his wry observations in books that included *The Hitchhiker's Guide to the Galaxy* and *The Restaurant at the End of the Universe.*[1] When Adams died in 2001, Richard Dawkins delivered a eulogy at the Church of Saint Martin in the Fields in London. "This next paragraph is one of Douglas's set-pieces," Dawkins said. "I heard it more than once, and I thought it was more brilliant every time."

Imagine a puddle waking up one morning and thinking, "This is an interesting world I find myself in—an interesting hole I find myself in. Fits me rather neatly, doesn't it? In fact it fits me staggeringly well—must have been made to have me in it!" This is such a powerful idea that as the sun rises in the sky and the air heats up and as, gradually, the puddle gets smaller and smaller, it's still frantically hanging on to the notion that everything's going to be alright, because this world was meant to have him in it, was built to have him in it; so the moment he disappears catches him rather by surprise. I think this may be something we need to be on the watch out for.[2]

Plenty of big, serious business books have shown how strongly the complacency and denial captured in Adams's metaphor correlate with corporate evaporation. The wise and influential business scholar Jagdish Sheth included complacency as one of seven deadly vices in his 2007 book, *The Self-Destructive Habits of Good Companies*.[3] In *Creative Destruction*, two McKinsey consultants using their company's massive corporate database demonstrated the dangers that arise when successful enterprises succumb to the ABCDs: arrogance, bureaucracy, complacency, and denial. Also instructive are books like *The Smartest Guys in the Room: The Amazing Rise and Scandalous Fall of Enron*,[4] and *When Genius Failed: The Rise and Fall of Long Term Capital Management*.[5]

But of course it doesn't require much deep reading in 2008 to see the ruinous consequences of complacency and denial, from the financial executives who thought that whatever they did was brilliantly clever and the corporate directors who acquiesced to that view, to the regulators who didn't see much need to regulate, to the individuals who somehow expected that living beyond their means was within their means.

And still, with all the warnings and all the experience, you could probably look around at work today and notice many places where complacency continues, substantially unabated—in managers who think their corner office was made to have them in it, in staff who disdain the extra effort required to fully satisfy a customer or strengthen a product, and in others who trot out the same old routines that got them where they are without realizing, or caring, that more is now required.

Few people have considered organizational inertia more thoroughly than John Kotter of the Harvard Business School. He begins his 2008 book, *A Sense of Urgency*, with the words "We are much too complacent. And we don't even know it."[6] (There's an important tipoff here to potential sources of misdirected organizational hubbub: As the Hall of Fame basketball coach Pat Riley has said, "When a great team loses through complacency, it will constantly search for new and more intricate explanations to explain away defeat.")

Kotter recommends four tactics for provoking the kind of healthy, non-frantic urgency that organizations require, the first of which is to "bring the outside in." Robert Heller, who studied the precipitous decline of IBM in the 1990s, recently observed:

> [I]nside IBM, almost everybody believed that they were working for the best of all possible companies, executing the best of all possible strategies in the best of all possible ways.
>
> This comforting and complacent inner view had been dangerously untrue for many years. For almost as long, a

quite different and far less flattering perception had been held by well-placed observers outside the company—including some important customers.[7]

More juicily than Kotter, but in the same vein, Heller says one way to combat complacency is to have "a mechanism that can rub insiders' noses in the truth of outsiders' perceptions."[8]

And then there's the matter of the truth of *insiders'* perceptions. In a 2007 study, 124 CEOs and 579 other senior executives were asked to evaluate the leadership dynamics within their organizations. Consistently, and dramatically, the non-CEOs rated things as being a whole lot worse than the CEOs believed them to be.

For example, while 52 percent of the non-CEOs said that their teams were doing poorly in critical areas such as thinking innovatively, leading change, cross-marketing, overseeing talent development, and building a company culture, just 28 percent of the CEOs reported problems in those areas. Here are some other results from the survey,[9] which used a one-to-seven scale:

	CEOs	Sr. Mgrs.
Team is effective overall	5.39	4.02
Decision-making processes are clear	5.62	3.86
Team deals well with conflict	4.98	3.73
CEO provides effective team direction	5.87	4.23

Comfy is good, and we all surely deserve some comfort in our demanding lives. Deluded, however, is dangerous.

Easter Island: From Comfortable to Dead

from *Get Out of Your Own Way*, by Robert Cooper[10]

Today Easter Island is a treeless wasteland with no living animals; but when the first Polynesians landed there it was quite the opposite: heavily forested and teeming with life, fertile enough to support a population as large as thirty thousand.

In order to erect the 900 huge stone statues that now form the island's only remaining "population," much wood was required: the Easter Islanders possessed neither wheels nor large animals, so each statue, after it was carved in a quarry, was dragged by hundreds of people on sledges made from tree trunks, using ropes made from other trees. As the trees disappeared, so did the rest of the island's vegetation and animal life, until there was nothing left to support the inhabitants.

"I have often asked myself," Jared Diamond writes, "'What did the Easter Islander who cut down the last palm tree say while he was doing it?'"[11]

And apparently no one, not even the quarriers, carvers, and sculptors who spent all day shaping rocks, thought to invent a wheel (reinvent it, really, since wheels had been invented in Mesopotamia four thousand years earlier). It's hard to imagine how much that single inspiration might have changed life on Easter Island—maybe, by preventing the island's deforestation, it might even have preserved the Easter Islanders from the descent into chaos and cannibalism that marked their civilization's last days.

As Malcolm Gladwell observes, "[S]ocieties, as often as not, aren't murdered. They commit suicide: they slit their wrists and then, in the course of many decades, stand by passively and watch themselves bleed to death."[12]

NOTES

1 Adams, Douglas. *The Hitchhiker's Guide to the Galaxy* (New York: Del Rey Books, 1995); *The Restaurant at the End of the Universe* (New York: Del Rey Books, 1995)

2 Dawkins, Richard. "Eulogy for Douglas Adams, Church of Saint Martin in the Fields, London. September 17, 2001." *Edge* at www.edge.org/documents/adams_index.html

3 Sheth, Jagdish. *The Self-Destructive Habits of Good Companies: … And How to Break Them* (Philadelphia: Wharton School Publishing, 2007)

4 McLean, Bethany, and Peter Elkind. (New York: Portfolio, 2003)

5 Lowenstein, Roger. (New York: Random House, 2001)

6 Kotter, John. *A Sense of Urgency.* (Cambridge, MA: Harvard Business Press, 2008)

7 Heller, Robert. "Complacency in Business: How Smugness and Complacency in Business Can Lead to Financial Crisis." *Edward de Bono and Robert Heller's Thinking Managers* at www.thinkingmanagers.com (www.thinkingmanagers.com/management/business-complacency.php)

8 Ibid.

9 Rosen, Richard, and Fred Adair. "CEOs Misperceive Top Teams' Performance." *Harvard Business Review* (September, 2007)

10 Cooper, Robert. *Get Out of Your Own Way: The 5 Keys to Surpassing Everyone's Expectations* (New York: Crown Books, 2006)

11 Diamond, Jared. *Collapse: How Societies Choose to Fail or Succeed* (New York: Viking, 2005)

12 Gladwell, Malcolm. "The Vanishing." *The New Yorker* (December 29, 2004). You can read this article at www.gladwell.com/2005/2005_01_15_a_collapse.html

Image source: "Puddle, UCLA, 2002" © Lim, Henry. See more at www.henrylim.org

SEE NEW NOW

The Fly in the Urinal

Maintaining focus can be a simple matter of having the right target.

Distressed by rundown conditions at New York's John F. Kennedy International Airport, the airport's owners turned its management over to the company that runs Amsterdam's Schiphol airport, renowned for its cleanliness and efficiency. Writing about the changes planned by that company, Schiphol USA, a *Wall Street*

Journal reporter explained:

> The tile under the urinals in the Arrivals Building [at JFK] has that familiar lemony tinge; rubber soles stick to it. Over in Amsterdam, the tile under Schiphol's urinals would pass inspection in an operating room. But nobody notices. What everybody does notice is that each urinal has a fly in it. Look harder, and the fly turns into the black outline of a fly, etched into the porcelain.
>
> "It improves the aim," says [a Schiphol official]. "If a man sees a fly, he aims at it." His staff conducted fly-in-urinal trials and found that the etchings reduce spillage by 80%.[1]

A simple reminder of an important business truth: having targets and paying attention to them makes a big difference.

It was Peter Drucker who, in 1945, coined the phrase "management by objectives" to describe that very process, which he viewed as an uncomplicated, even self-evident, exercise: set targets and then manage in a way to reach those targets.[2]

Of course, it didn't take long for squadrons of symbiotic consultants, academics, and human-resource experts to make management by objectives, or MBO, so complicated, time-consuming, forms-laden, finicky, and tedious that nearly everyone came to hate it.[3] This progression comports with Eric Hoffer's observation, "Every great cause begins as a movement, degenerates into a business and ends up as a racket."[4]

Judging from the state of today's most advanced urinals, overcomplication is just the way of the world. Now there's the "On

Target" urinal, which has a pressure-sensitive screen recessed into it, so the user can score points by shooting moving images onscreen.[5]

And the talking urinal cake, which the state government of New Mexico purchased and provided to bars and restaurants. "Hey there, big guy. Having a few drinks?" a female voice says a few seconds after a motion sensor in the device is activated. "It's time to call a cab or ask a sober friend for a ride home."[6] And, sadly, much more.[7]

Whatever happened to keeping it simple, stupid?

Men, Aiming, and "The Golf Gene"

from "The Golf Gene," by John Tierney[8]

Golf features no body contact, no car crashes and no cheerleaders, yet men keep watching. They make up more than 80 percent of the TV audience for golf. This might simply be because they like watching a game they play themselves; men make up nearly 80 percent of the golfers in America, too. But then why do so many guys play such a frustrating game?...

Was golf the modern version of Pleistocene hunting on the savanna? The notion had already occurred to devotees of evolutionary psychology, as I discovered from reading Edward O. Wilson and Steve Sailer. They point to surveys and other research showing that people in widely different places and cultures have a common vision of what makes a beautiful landscape—and it looks a lot like the view from golfers' favorite tees.

The ideal is a vista from high ground overlooking open, rolling grassland dotted with low-branched trees and a body of water. It would have been a familiar and presumably pleasant view for ancient hunters: an open savanna where prey could be spotted as they grazed; a water hole to attract animals; trees offering safe hiding places for hunters.

The descendants of those hunters seem to have inherited their fascination with hitting targets, because today's men excel at tests asking them to predict the flights of projectiles. They also seem to get a special pleasure from watching such flights, both in video games and real life. No matter how many times male pilots have seen a plane land, they'll watch another one just for the satisfaction of seeing the trajectory meet the ground.

That's the only plausible excuse for watching golf. Men, besides having a primal affection for the vistas of fairways, get so much joy watching that little ball fly toward the green that they'll sit through everything else. One sight of a putt dropping in the hole makes up for long moments watching pudgy guys agonize over which club to use.

NOTES

1 Newman, Barry. "Apple Turnover: Dutch Are Invading JFK Arrivals Building And None Too Soon—U.S.'s Best-Known Airport Has Been a Lousy Place To Land, Walk or Stand—Using Flies to Help Fliers." *Wall Street Journal* (May 13, 1997)

2 Greenwood, Ronald. "Management by Objectives: As Developed by Peter Drucker, Assisted by Harold Smiddy." *Academy of Management Review* (April, 1981).

3 Not everyone, though. According to *The Economist* magazine, "George [W.] Bush is a devotee of Mr Drucker's idea of 'management by objectives.' ('I had read Peter Drucker,' Karl Rove once told the *Atlantic Monthly*, 'but I'd never *seen* Drucker until I saw Bush in action.')" From "Peter Drucker." *The Economist* (November 17, 2005)

4 Hoffer, Eric. *The True Believer: Thoughts on the Nature of Mass*

Movements (New York: Time-Life Books, 1980)

5 http://www.gadgetreview.com/2006/03/video-game-urinal.html

6 _____. "Urinals Speak Out Against DWI." *Albuquerque Tribune* (February 12, 2007)

7 For example, the "World Cup Urinal." at http://www.idiotworld.com/story/583/Soccer_Urinal

8 Tierney, John. "The Golf Gene." *New York Times* (August 20, 2005). You can read the full article at http://www.nytimes.com/2005/08/20/opinion/20tierney.html?_r=1

SEE NEW NOW

Spencer's Warbler

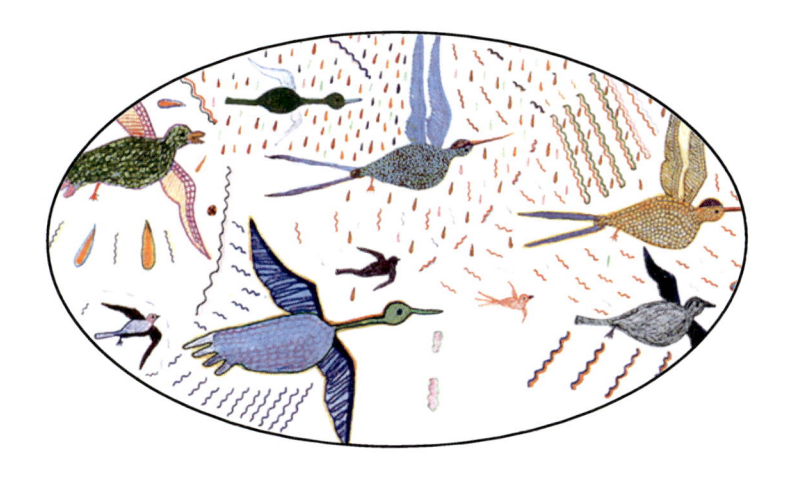

There's a big difference between knowing the name of something and knowing something.

Richard Feynman was a scientific genius, a Nobel Prize-winning physicist. He became best known to a generation of Americans when during the investigation of the space shuttle *Challenger* disaster he dropped some of the craft's insulating material (from what was referred to as an "O-ring") into a glass of ice water to show that it could not withstand freezing temperatures.

Feynman's fun-loving nature has been documented in books that include *Surely You're Joking, Mr. Feynman!*[1] Fellow science genius Freeman Dyson once wrote that Feynman was "half-genius, half-buffoon," but later changed that to "all-genius, all-buffoon."[2]

Feynman would often explain his distinctive mental capacities through an anecdote involving his father, Melvin. The father and his young son would take long walks together, and Richard would ask a typical child's questions. He remembered asking his father the name of a bird, and his father answering him—although his father had no idea of the bird's actual name in any language—as follows:

> It's a Spencer's warbler... Well, in Italian, it's a chutto Lapittida. In Portuguese, it's a Bom da Peida. In Chinese, it's a Chung-long-tah, and in Japanese, it's a Katano Tekeda. You can know the name of that bird in all the languages of the world, but when you're finished, you'll know absolutely nothing whatever about the bird. You'll only know about humans in different places, and what they call the bird. So let's look at the bird and see what it's doing—that's what counts.[3]

"I learned very early," Feynman wrote, "the difference between knowing the name of something and knowing something."[4]

Much of education consists of learning the correct names for things, or at least good, acceptable names for things. The danger occurs when the names replace, rather than enhance, understanding. Chicago attorney Gilbert Cornfield heads a successful firm with his name on the door and many attorneys inside. "In law school," Cornfield says, "you learn to give names to problems and then deal with them based on the names: 'This is a contracts problem, this an intellectual property problem,' and so on. But every legal problem is about some particular people in some particular circumstances, with some particular history. Unless you understand those things, you can 'do your job,' but you're not actually serving the real needs of your clients."[5]

Expertise, let us emphasize, is not bad. But expertise that categorizes things in limiting or even inaccurate ways, so that important information is missed or alternatives are excluded, is dangerous. Is there a word in the business vocabulary that has been more venerated over the years than "productivity"? Yet Henry Mintzberg, the dean of business scholars, declared in the *Harvard Business Review*, "Productivity is killing American enterprise." "I fear for the future of American business," he wrote,

> not because of U.S. trade imbalances or budget deficits but because of the productivity of its corporations. America's highly touted productivity may be destroying its legendary enterprise and many of its powerful enterprises... For the sake of American society, as well as the American economy, it is time to get past productivity.[6]

In the name of productivity, Mintzberg argued, too many American companies are "trading away their future health for short-term results." Slavishly honoring the word, without considering what's behind it, is counterproductive.

There's a name for learning and labeling that limit understanding and awareness rather than expanding them: "educated incapacity." Marketing consultant Edith Weiner has defined educated incapacity as "knowing so much about what you know that you're the last to be able to see the future for it differently."[7] Business author William Altier here introduces one of many thousands of possible examples:

> Collectively, the major automakers must have thousands of

engineers on their payrolls, and it's probably safe to say that most of them drive cars and that they must have driven in the rain. Thus they must have experienced the exasperation of continually having to turn their windshield wipers on and off during a light rainfall.[8]

He's referring, of course, to the invention of intermittent wipers, which were first developed not by an auto company engineer but by a college professor, and first put into use at Ford the late 1970s.[9] The auto company engineers probably had made hundreds of small improvements to windshield wiper arms, blades, and motors over many years, yet none of them perceived a fundamental shortcoming in the way auto drivers experienced them. Wipers, not customers' experiences—not even their own experiences as customers—were what they worried about.

To bring fresh perspectives, some organizations are using ethnography—viewing particular interactions with the eyes of an anthropologist—to tackle critical tasks in ways that go beyond traditional categories. Thomas Kelley, general manager of the vaunted design firm IDEO, describes the anthropologist's perspective as a core thinking skill employed at his firm.[10] He says, "Others approach a problem from the point of view that says, 'We have the smartest people in the world; therefore, we can think this through.' We approach it from the point of view that the answer is out there, hidden in plain sight, so let's go observe human behavior and see where the opportunities are."[11]

Alegent Health System in Omaha studied cancer patients ethnographically to determine what they perceived as critical factors in their experience of treatment. Discovering that when those patients looked better they felt better, Alegent implemented a first-of-its-kind Image Recovery Center, a hospital-based program employing clinically trained cosmetologists to help patients prepare for and redress appearance changes they experience due to chemotherapy, radiation therapy, or surgery.[12] The program has won national awards and now is being emulated at other hospitals and cancer centers.

Karen Stephenson is a trained anthropologist who helps organizations see themselves in fresh ways. Her company, Netform, develops graphical depictions of information flows, showing among other things who are the company's gatekeepers, hubs, and pulsetakers. You could see her as a "communication" specialist, but as her 2008 book[13] shows, she is as much a specialist in trust and other disciplines. Hire a typical "trust" expert and you're likely to get workshops and lectures; hiring Stephenson or someone with similar skills could mean that you might get a fuller, fresher understanding of the dynamics underlying trust in your organization, so you can make change that is systemic, not superficial.

Call whatever you're observing or thinking about "Spencer's warbler" and then look to see what's really happening, and you might improve your decision-making in important ways.

New Lenses—An Anthropologist's View
from *Available Light* by Clifford Geertz[14]

[A]nthropology has played, in our day, a vanguard role. We have been the first to insist on a number of things: that the world does not divide into the pious and the superstitious; that there are sculptures in jungles and paintings in deserts; that political order is possible without centralized power and principled justice without codified rules; that the norms of reason were not fixed in Greece, the evolution of morality not consummated in England. Most important, we were the first to insist that we see the lives of others through lenses of our own grinding and that they look back on ours through ones of their own.

NOTES

1 Feynman, Richard and Ralph Leighton. *Surely You're Joking, Mr. Feynman! (Adventures of a Curious Character)* (New York: Norton, 1997)

2 Sykes, Richard. Preface to *No Ordinary Genius: The Illustrated Richard Feynman* (New York: Norton, 1996)

3 Olson, Steve. *Inquiry and National Science Education Standards* (Washington, D.C.: National Academies Press, 2000)

4 Feynman, Richard, and Ralph Leighton. *What Do You Care What Other People Think? Further Adventures of A Curious Character* (New York: Norton, 2001)

5 Cornfield, Gilbert. "Centennial Address: Lawyering as Service to People." Santa Cruz, California (March 8, 2008)

6 Mintzberg, Henry. "Productivity Is Killing American Enterprise." *Harvard Business Review* (July-August, 2007)

7 Weiner, Edith. "Ten Thinking Technologies." Presentation at The Masters Forum (September 14, 2004). You can read a summary of that presentation at www.seenewnow.com/summaries/weiner.pdf. See also her book (with Arnold Brown), *FutureThink: How to Think Clearly in a Time of Change* (Englewood Cliffs, NJ: Prentice Hall, 2005)

8 Altier, William. *The Thinking Manager's Toolbox: Effective Processes for Problem Solving and Decision Making* (New York: Oxford University Press, 1999)

9 "Robert Kearns, Inventor of Intermittent Wipers, Dies at 77." *USA Today* (February 25, 2005)

10 Kelley, Thomas, and Jonathon Littman. *The Ten Faces of Innovation: IDEO's Strategies for Defeating the Devil's Advocate and Driving Creativity Throughout Your Organization* (New York: Doubleday Business, 2005)

11 Pethokoukus, James. "The Deans of Design." *U.S. News & World Report* (September 24, 2006). You can read this article at www.usnews.com/usnews/biztech/articles/060924/2best.htm.

12 _____. "Surviving Cancer is a Life-long Process." *HER* (June-July, 2007) You can read this article at www.omahapublications.com/legends/hercancerarticle.php.

13 Stephenson, Karen. *A Quantum Theory of Trust: The Secrets of Mapping and Managing Human Relationships* (New York: Financial Times Prentice Hall, 2008). You can read more about her thinking in Kleiner, Art, "Karen Stephenson's Quantum Theory of Trust," *Strategy+Business* (Fourth Quarter, 2002), at www.strategy-business.com/press/16635507/20964

14 Geertz, Clifford. *Available Light: Anthropological Reflections On Philosophical Topics* (Princeton, NJ: Princeton University Press, 2000)

Image: Papialuk, Josie Pamiutu. (also, Papealook) "Different Kinds of Birds" (detail)

SEE NEW NOW

The Twenty-Dollar-Bill Auction

Look before you leap. Then look again.

Max Bazerman teaches negotiation at Harvard Business School. He is the author, co-author, or co-editor of sixteen books, including the 2007 *Negotiation Genius*,[1] and over 180 research articles and chapters.

He began his Masters Forum presentation[2] by auctioning off a twenty-dollar bill. Conducting such auctions has been very lucrative for him. He has written:

> I have sold a $20 bill for $407, and I have had eleven $20 auctions hit the $100 mark. I once sold a $100 bill for $505. In total, I have earned over $20,000 running these auctions in classes over the last decade (which I have used to throw a class party, or donated to charity).[3]

Yes, people pay more than twenty dollars for an ordinary twenty-dollar bill. Executives, MBA students—smart people, who you'd think would be wiser than that. They're not deceived by Bazerman in any way—they just become ensnared in poor judgment.

In the auctions as Bazerman conducts them, with the rules clearly stated from the beginning, the high bidder wins the twenty dollars, but the runner-up bidder has to pay, too: whatever his or her last bid was. It's a sucker's game, or an "enticement" game, as economists call it. Bazerman describes it as embodying "the tyranny of small steps." People get into the bidding, and then they can't—or at least they won't—get out, even as it quickly becomes clear that the escalating dynamics mean that the "winner" will pay more than twenty dollars for that bill, but the loser will pay almost as much and get nothing.[4] Things then come down to two people playing chicken, each hoping the other will cut and run.

Bazerman says he's conducted this auction several hundred times, and there have been fewer than five occasions when the winner paid less than the bill was worth.

Let this be a lens about not digging yourself ever deeper into any untenable holes, small step by small step. About that often-quoted saying that's usually attributed to one Native American source or another: "If you find yourself riding a dead horse, the best strategy is to dismount."

Writers have observed this auction's counterproductive dynamics at work in areas that include college athletics,[5] labor negotiations,[6] campaign-finance reform,[7] and branding battles,[8] among others.

In their bestseller *Blue Ocean Strategy*, Chan Kim and Renée Mauborgne[9] challenge leaders to find wide-open competitive spaces (blue oceans) where margins are huge and competitors are scarce or nonexistent, in contrast to "red oceans" where businesses too often "accept the constraining factors of war—limited terrain and the need to defeat an enemy in order to succeed."[10] You can't get much more "red ocean" than the twenty-dollar-bill auction.

Plenty of personal applications here, too. Maybe you'll see some relationship parallels to the organizational behaviors Bazerman has described:

> We find that many executives tend to continue a competitive strategy beyond the point that it makes sense, in order to justify a situation that they have gotten themselves into. At some point, when the competitors start losing money, they get mad at each other, at which point all they care about is beating each other.[11]

It takes two people to escalate the twenty-dollar-bill auction from an apparent opportunity to a financial death spiral. Either one of them, with only a small loss, could stop the damage, but most often their sense of self-regard, their fear of losing face, their redirected anger, or just plain cussedness pushes them on, to the point where they both will lose and it's only a matter of how much. The twenty-dollar-bill auction is a lesson to look before you leap, but be willing to look after you've leapt, too.

The $25,000 Twenty-Dollar Bill

An ordinary fruit sticker that mysteriously ended up on a twenty-dollar bill has inspired big-bucks auctions of its own. The flawed bill, sometimes called "the banana note," bears a red, green, and yellow Del Monte sticker next to Andrew Jackson's portrait.

Here's the story as told at Delmontenote.com:[12]

> The twenty-dollar bill went through the entire Bureau of Engraving and Printing inspection checkpoints until it finally found itself sitting in an ATM Machine somewhere in the state of Ohio.
>
> There, a young college student retrieved it and immediately realized he had a $20.00 bill worth more than face value. No one knows what steps he took to market his new find, but it is verified that he found E-bay as a profitable outlet.
>
> He listed it for auction and it caught the eye of a collector from Phoenix, Arizona by the name of Daniel Wishnatsky. He won the bid for $10,100.00 in 2003. Not a bad profit for going to the ATM!
>
> Daniel Wishnatsky is a member of the Society of Paper Money Collectors. He felt the Del Monte Note™ should bring two to three times that amount. He was on the money. In January 2006 he placed the famous bill for auction with the notable Heritage Galleries.

In a small town outside of Fort Worth, Texas Jackie Morales was enjoying his usual breakfast of biscuits and gravy at a fast food restaurant when he read about the twenty-dollar bill worth over $10,000.00. Like Mr. Wishnatsky, he too thought it was worth two or three times more.

Jackie went back to his business, Texas RV Center Inc., and spoke with his wife Bethany. They both agreed that the Del Monte Note™ would be a wise investment.

$25,300.00 later, the happy Morales couple claimed it as theirs. When the Moraleses were asked what their plans for the Del Monte Note™ were, Bethany replied, "It's an investment. We would of course sell it if the right offer came up but in the meantime we are going to enjoy owning the only one in existence."

NOTES

1 Bazerman, Max, and Deepak Malhotra. *Negotiation Genius: How to Overcome Obstacles and Achieve Brilliant Results at the Bargaining Table and Beyond* (New York: Bantam Books, 2007)

2 Bazerman, Max. "What Is Strategy?" Presentation at The Masters Forum (November 2, 1994)

3 Bazerman, Max. *Smart Money Decisions: Why You Do What You Do With Money (And How to Change for the Better)* (New York: Wiley, 2001). Bazerman has recently upped the ante in his bidding game from twenty dollars to 100 dollars.

4 The bidding proceeds in one-dollar increments. Say that several people enter the bidding in the early stages. Those who remain in the bidding believe that since presumably no one will bid more than twenty dollars for a twenty-dollar bill, they will win it for some lower amount. But (limiting the description to only two people), when someone bids nineteen dollars, someone else who has bid

eighteen dollars now stands to lose that whole amount. The person at eighteen dollars will then bid twenty dollars, in order to break even rather than losing the entire eighteen. But now the person who bid nineteen dollars is in the same boat: s/he can give up and lose the entire nineteen dollars, or bid twenty-one dollars and hope to lose only one dollar. That puts the shoe back on the foot of the person who bid twenty dollars: lose it all or bid twenty-two dollars in hopes of losing only two dollars. And so it goes.

5 Latz, Martin. *Gain the Edge!* (New York: St. Martin's Press, 2005)

6 Beamer, Glenn, and David Lewis. "The Irrational Escalation of Commitment and the Ironic Labor Politics of the Rust Belt." *Enterprise & Society* (December, 2003)

7 Landsburg, Steven. "Party Tricks: Twenty Dollar Bills and Campaign Finance Reform" *Slate* (November 6, 1998) at www.slate.com/id/7103

8 Finley, Michael. "Max Bazerman: Session Review." You can read Finley's account of this presentation at http://mfinley.com/experts/bazerman/bazerman.htm. At this website you can also read many other summaries of Masters Forum presentations.

9 Mauborgne spoke at The Masters Forum in 2006. You can read a summary of her presentation at www.seenewnow.com/summaries/mauborgne.pdf.

10 Kim, Chan, and Renée Mauborgne. *Blue Ocean Strategy: How to Create Uncontested Market Space and Make the Competition Irrelevant* (Boston: Harvard Business School Press, 2005)

11 Bazerman, Max. "What Is Strategy?" Presentation at The Masters Forum (November 2, 1994)

12 "The History of the Famous Del Monte Note" at www.delmontenote.com

The Stirrup

Next thing you know, the world's a different place. Will you see it in time?

The world underwent a big change in the Middle Ages, when feudalism took hold throughout Europe. In the feudalistic structure, a lord who owned land granted possession of some of that land (which was called a "feud" or a "fief") to vassals, who agreed in return to provide military service to the lord. Feudalism created a coherent social structure, new legal systems, a source of armies for defense and conquest, and many other outcomes.

But what brought feudalism into being? Historian Lynn White says it was the stirrup. "Few inventions have been so simple as the stirrup," he wrote, "but few have had so catalytic an influence on history."[1]

Harvard Business School professor Richard Tedlow summarized White's argument while addressing a conference on the future of the internet:

> Before the stirrup, the horse was basically a mechanism to get a javelin thrower around, but with the stirrup, you could brace yourself on the horse and thrust forward. So all of a sudden the horse becomes the atomic weapon of the eighth century and now the troops need horses, the horses need fodder, fodder requires land, land requires someone to work it, and the result is feudalism. Nobody said, "Now, what I need is feudalism. What I think I'll invent is a stirrup."[2]

Tedlow added, "Nothing came down from the sky and said, 'Hey, you idiots, this is a whole new paradigm.'"

One writer described the stirrup's consequences in the following way:

> [T]here is no doubt that the stirrup enabled new forms of warfare... Success in those forms of warfare changed who ruled and who perished. The languages we speak, the food on our table, the system of government we use, and even our genetic makeup were affected. All from a few bits of metal and leather weighing around 600 grams. It changed our world.[3]

You might let those few bits of metal and leather serve as a reminder that the most profound strategies can sometimes be the simplest. When Larry Keeley, president of the Doblin Group and recognized as one of today's most influential innovation consultants, spoke at The Masters Forum, he said this about strategy:

> A great strategy has a single major point: It says what you are going to do to constructively alter the daily lives of millions of people... Unfortunately, the people who craft strategy usually aren't curious enough about peoples' everyday lives. Yet that is always the best starting place for true breakthroughs... You'd be amazed at how much of innovation is just a matter of paying really close attention to people. You learn what people want from what they actually do—not what they say, not what the planners imagine, and not what the technologists assume.[4]

"The guy who invented the first wheel was an idiot. The guy who invented the other three, he was a genius," said the comedian Sid Caesar. A certain truth to that witticism (although of course the wheel, singular, has many uses in technological applications: the first wheel was probably a potter's wheel), and it's interesting to note that although the first use of the wheel for transportation was on Mesopotamian chariots around 3200 BCE,[5] many advanced civilizations never developed wheels for transportation applications. In the Mayan world there were wheels on some children's toys, but they never were put to use in other ways.

Sometimes great, simple ideas are right there in front of your nose, and you miss them—and a revolution proceeds without you.

How much might you miss by not paying attention to everyday things? *Financial Times* and the *Washington Post*, among others, have credited social media with a major part in Barack Obama's virtually out-of-nowhere race past Hillary Clinton to become the Democratic Party's presidential nominee on the way to becoming President. In just the first two months of 2008, Obama spent roughly $3.5 million on internet media, while Clinton spent about $350,000. Obama raised $91 million in that way; Clinton raised $37 million.

For this lens, here is the central point:

> Political consultants who specialize in online fundraising say Obama has, in two months, rewritten the rules for raising campaign cash. "Anytime you can reach a million donors with the click of a mouse, you redefine the way campaign finance is done in American politics," said [a political strategist][6]

Obama's advisors understood how this "stirrup" worked best, and they used it to transform their operations. One observer noted, "Even businesses find it hard to change their organizational structure to fit the demands of new technology. But for political campaigns, which are classic command-and-control operations, it is particularly difficult. Mrs. Clinton maintains a competent and solid website but Mr. Obama has made it the central organizing tool of his campaign."[7]

Summing things up, *The Economist* wrote, "Mrs. Clinton built the best fund-raising machine of the 20th century... But Mr. Obama trumped her by building the best fund-raising machine of the 21st century."[8]

In his best-seller *The Black Swan*, Nassim Nicholas Taleb cautioned against the curveballs that life throws at those who try to use a command and control strategy to make the future in the way they want it to be, rather than the way it's going to be regardless of their efforts. In an interview, he urged "tinkering" as the best business strategy to avoid the unanticipated occurrences he refers to as "black swans":

> Trial and error will save us from ourselves because they capture benign black swans. Look at the three big inventions of our time: lasers, computers and the internet. They were all produced by tinkering and none of them ended up doing what their inventors intended them to do. All were black swans. The big hope for the world is that, as we tinker, we have a capacity for choosing the best outcomes.[9]

Taleb's advice for managing personal finances could apply to many other aspects of life as well: "[T]he good investment strategy is to put 90% of your money in the safest possible government securities and the remaining 10% in a large number of high-risk ventures. This insulates you from bad black swans and exposes you to the possibility of good ones."[10]

Marshall McLuhan said, "We shape our tools and they in turn shape us." Are you really open to all the game-changing opportunities in your business and personal worlds, or does, just maybe, a "command-and-control" mentality or some other way of being keep you from creating simple developments that can lead to big gains?

The End of the Knight on Horseback

from "How the Stirrup Changed Our World," by Dan Derby[11]

> Only the adoption of another amazingly simple innovation would bring the mounted warrior down. Sometime in the thirteenth century, the English adopted "Five and a half feet

of European Yew wood...about two pounds," better known as the English longbow. Allowing striking distances several orders of magnitude beyond the mounted knight's lance, it also countered his heavy armor with its penetrating power.... In early battles, kill ratios (archers vs. enemy soldiers) of 1000 to 1 were not uncommon. With a range of nearly an eighth of a mile, the English longbow became the most feared weapon on earth. By any comparison, it was cheap to build and cheap to man. Overnight, it would dominate warfare and its users would dominate their lands.

NOTES

1 For White's famously brilliant scholarly discourse on the relationship between the stirrup and feudalism, see his *Medieval Technology and Social Change* (Oxford University Press, 1966)

2 "The Evolution and Future of the Internet," *Hamilton Consultants Newsletter* (5th edition, 1998) at www.hamiltonco.com/features/hampub/news5.pdf

3 Derby, Dan. "How the Stirrup Changed Our World." *StrangeHorizons* (September 24, 2001) at www.strangehorizons.com/2001/20010924/stirrup.shtml

4 Keeley, Larry. "Why So Glum, Chum? Secrets of Breakout Innovation." Presentation at The Masters Forum (November 12, 2003)

5 This is the commonly-accepted date and location for the invention of the wheel, although research at sites in Russia and Kazakhstan suggests earlier dates. See Wilford, John. "Remaking the Wheel: Evolution of the Chariot." *New York Times* (February 22, 1994)

6 Mosk, Matthew. "Obama Rewriting Rules for Raising Campaign

Money Online." *Washington Post* (March 28, 2008)

7 Peter Leyden, quoted in Luce, Edward. "Obama Steals A March With Technology." *Financial Times* (February 20 2008)

8 _____. "The Fall of the House of Clinton." *The Economist* (June 5, 2008)

9 Appleyard, Bryan. "Nassim Nicholas Taleb: The Prophet of Boom and Doom." *The Sunday Times (London)* (June 1, 2008)

10 Ibid.

11 Derby, Dan. Op. cit. (See note 3)

Image source: "Bayeux Tapestry, Bayeux."Personal picture taken by Urban" (February 2005), upgraded by Tatoute (December 2005). Wikimedia Commons. The scene depicted is from the Battle of Hastings in 1066. The tapestry was created within just a few years after the historic battle. To read more, see Grape, Wolfgang, *The Bayeux Tapestry* (New York: Prestel-Verlag, 1994)

SEE NEW NOW

The Caterpillar

Transformation isn't always as glorious as it's made out to be.

Harvard Business School professor Anthony Athos was prolific and influential. He co-authored *The Art of Japanese Management* with Richard Pascale,[1] popularizing the 7-S model that has become one of the most useful tools for looking in an integrated way at how prepared an organization is to carry out its strategy.[2]

James Champy, co-author of *Reengineering the Corporation*,[3] admired Athos for his brilliance and for his wisdom. "Tony was perceptive, deep, and a realist," Champy has said. "He understood organizational dysfunction so well that it pained him, and he eventually stopped consulting."[4]

When Athos appeared at The Masters Forum, he used the lens of the caterpillar's metamorphosis into a butterfly to make an important point about transformational change:

> What about the caterpillar? You're going about your business, you've got all these little legs and they all can walk and you don't fall down and you know how to eat green leaves. You're really good at it; you're just fat and furry and you're really a competent caterpillar. And then somebody comes along and tells you it's time to transform yourself. The caterpillar says, "Why would I want to do that?"
>
> And he weaves this little thing around himself, and as the light goes down, every time he weaves the little thing more, he begins to notice that his legs are falling off, and that he's drying out and rotting, and at some moment it all goes black. But when the butterfly emerges—finally, there is a flutter, unless something goes very wrong—he doesn't even remember the caterpillar at all. You've got to get that.[5]

It's easy to get excited in an abstract way about transformation. Here's the business philosopher Peter Koestenbaum linking it to greatness:

> [T]he pursuit of greatness is what makes life worth living, or dying for.... Let me give you a second word to use: transformation. Greatness has to do with the seduction, the attractiveness of transformation: What would it mean if I were

to shift my primary value from being ordinary to extraordinary? This is the hero's journey.[6]

In organizations, that kind of abstract excitement about transformation has been referred to as "planning euphoria." But making it happen is another matter. Athos's caterpillar provides a nice metaphor for what it's like to really transform, at a deep level.

If you want to sink into the metaphor, author Susun Weed takes the specifics a little farther: "Within that cocoon, the caterpillar does not just lose a few legs and grow wings, the caterpillar melts down. The caterpillar actually turns to goo or slime, and then has to rebuild into a butterfly."[7] That's a valuable antidote to euphoria, important to remember particularly when you're asking others to undertake deep change.

Athos's other point, the one about which he says "You've got to get that," is perhaps a bit less obvious. Psychologists tell us that any change, even one acknowledged to be for the better, can bring with it a deep sense of loss, even grief. Most of us want, in some deep way, to remember the caterpillar. We don't say, "I weigh a hundred and twenty-five pounds now," we say, "I've lost thirty pounds!" We don't want people just to say, "You run such an efficient, friendly office," we want them to acknowledge the work and ingenuity and perseverance it took to make it that way: how much worse it was before.

And that's something that people always fear about organizational transformation: that all they have accomplished, all they've been through, personally and professionally, will be forgotten or at least disregarded, leaving them to wish they had remained as competent caterpillars.

Profound, transformative changes to things as we know them

may be the order of the day, and leaders may need to make them. But it is unwise to forget the caterpillar while doing so.

Nabokov's Butterflies

The novelist Vladimir Nabokov was a passionate lepidopterist. He wrote the following for students in a literature class he taught at Cornell:[8]

> Transformation is a marvelous thing. I am thinking especially of the transformation of butterflies. Though wonderful to watch, transformation from larva to pupa or from pupa to butterfly is not a particularly pleasant process for the subject involved....
>
> In the last hours, the pupa splits as the caterpillar had split—it is really a last glorified moult, and the butterfly creeps out—and in its turn hangs down from the twig to dry. She is not handsome at first. She is very damp and bedraggled. But those limp implements of hers that she has disengaged gradually dry, distend, the veins branch and harden—and in twenty minutes or so she is ready to fly. You have noticed that the caterpillar is a *he,* the pupa an *it,* and the butterfly a *she.* You will ask—what is the feeling of hatching? Oh, no doubt, there is a rush of panic to the head, a thrill of breathless and strange sensation, but then the eyes see, in a flow of sunshine, the butterfly sees the world, the large and awful face of the gaping entomologist.

NOTES

1 Athos, Anthony, and Richard Pascale. *The Art of Japanese Management: Applications for American Executives* (New York: Simon & Schuster, 1981). Among other things, Athos also coauthored the influential 1993 *Harvard Business Review* article, "The Reinvention Roller Coaster: Risking the Present for a Powerful Future," with Pascale and Tracey Goss.

2 You can read more about the 7-S Model in Waterman, Robert, Thomas Peters, and Julien Phillips, "Structure is Not Organization—The 7-S Framework." *Business Horizons* (June 1980), and at many online sites, including here: www.mindtools.com/pages/article/newSTR_91.

3 Champy, James, and Michael Hammer. *Reengineering the Corporation: A Manifesto for Business Revolution* (revised edition) (New York: Collins Business Essentials, 2003)

4 Dearlove, Dess, and Stuart Crainer. "Whatever Happened to Yesterday's Bright Ideas?" *The Conference Board Review* (May/June, 2006)

5 Athos, Anthony (with Richard Pascale). "Reinvention." Presentation at The Masters Forum (September 9, 1995)

6 Koestenbaum, Peter. "The Leadership Diamond." Presentation at The Masters Forum (September 14, 1993). You can read more of Koestenbaum's thoughts at www.pib.net.

7 Weed, Susun, interviewed by Randy Peyser. "Menopause as an Earth Changing Experience." At www.randypeyser.com

8 Nabokov, Vladimir, in "Nabokov's Butterflies" (introduction by Brian Boyd). *The Atlantic Monthly* (April, 2000). You can read this article at www.theatlantic.com/issues/2000/04/nabokov.htm.